Physical Science

BY

MYRL SHIREMAN

COPYRIGHT © 1997 Mark Twain Media, Inc.

1–58037–023–3

Printing No. CD–1820

Mark Twain Media, Inc., Publishers
Distributed by Carson-Dellosa Publishing Company, Inc.

Introduction

When compared to students on an international basis, middle-school students in the United States do not generally score well in understanding physical science concepts. Additionally, data shows that in the United States, males are more likely to continue the study of physical science than females. This book is designed specifically to encourage male and female middle-school students as they develop some of the important concepts associated with physical science.

The activities included in this book are developed around some of the major physical science concepts. Since vocabulary development is so important to understanding physical science concepts, the activities are designed so students can become familiar with the physical science vocabulary. Problem-solving activities are included to encourage students and give them many opportunities to solve problems that are associated with the important concepts. Additionally, there are activities that let the students speculate about possible solutions. These help develop predicting and reasoning skills.

Table of Contents

Name _____ Date _____

Understanding Matter

To understand physical science, you must understand **matter**. Matter is shared by all objects. Matter refers to what an object is made of. Two terms that are important in learning about matter are **mass** and **weight**. All matter has mass and weight.

Mass refers to the amount of matter in an object. Unless an object gains or loses matter, the amount of matter remains constant. Whether an object is above the earth's surface or on the earth's surface, the mass remains constant.

Weight refers to the force with which gravity attracts an object. Weight and mass are often confused; therefore, it is important to remember that weight is a force that changes if an object is moved from the surface of the earth to some distance above the earth. Mass does not change; it is the same on or above the earth's surface.

Each of the following statements has an error. Read the statement and correct the error on the blanks below the statement.

1. Mass and weight are the same thing.

_____

_____

2. The mass of an object is greater on the earth's surface than it is 1,000 feet above the earth's surface.

_____

_____

3. An object on the earth's surface may have mass, but it does not have weight.

_____

_____

Name _____ Date _____

MEASUREMENT OF MASS

In science, you will find that the **English system** or the **metric system** may be used for the measurement of mass. The terms *ounce* and *pound* are English measurements used to measure the mass of an object. In the metric system, the terms *gram* and *kilogram* are used when measuring the mass of an object.

metric system
gram
kilogram

English system
ounce
pound

In the metric system, mass is measured as so many grams (g) or kilograms. The mass of smaller objects is best measured in grams. One kilogram equals **1,000** grams. One kilogram equals 2.2 pounds. Four hundred fifty-four grams (454 g) equals one pound.

Complete the following chart.

CHART I

	GRAMS	=	KILOGRAMS	=	POUNDS
1.	1,000	=	1	=	2.2
2.	2,000	=	_____	=	_____
3.	3,000	=	_____	=	_____
4.	3,500	=	_____	=	_____
5.	_____	=	4	=	_____
6.	_____	=	6.5	=	_____
7.	_____	=	_____	=	17.6
8.	500	=	1/2	=	_____
9.	100	=	1/____	=	_____
10.	_____	=	1/1,000	=	_____

Name _____ Date _____

MEASUREMENT OF WEIGHT

Weight refers to how gravity affects an object. Although the mass of an object remains constant, the weight of an object is not constant. An object with the same mass will weigh more on the surface of the earth than in outer space. The farther an object is from the center of the earth, the less it will weigh.

Gravity affects the weight of an object, but it does not affect the mass of an object. However, the gravitational pull of an object is related to the mass of the object. The greater the mass, the greater the gravitational attraction. The gravitational attraction (weight) of an object on earth is greater than the gravitational attraction (weight) of an object on Mars.

To understand gravity, you must think of your weight registered as a force pulling you toward the center of the earth. There is also a force pushing back against you. Weight registers because the force of gravity is pulling you against the scale, which is held firm by the floor.

The weight of an object is measured in **dynes** and **newtons**. The symbol for newton is (N). An object with one gram is attracted to the earth with a gravitational force of 980 dynes. One hundred thousand (100,000) dynes equals one newton (N).

Complete the following chart.

CHART II

	GRAMS		DYNES
1.	1	=	980
2.	10	=	_____
3.	50	=	_____
4.	100	=	_____
5.	1,000	=	_____

Answer the following:

6. One thousand grams equals one kilogram. One kilogram equals _____ dynes.

7. One hundred thousand dynes equals one newton (N). One kilogram equals _____ newtons (N).

Complete the following chart.

CHART III

	KILOGRAMS		NEWTONS
8.	1	=	9.8
9.	10	=	_____
10.	100	=	_____
11.	500	=	_____
12.	1,000	=	_____

Name _____ Date _____

MEASUREMENT OF WEIGHT (CONTINUED)

One pound equals 4.5 newtons (N).

Complete the following chart.

CHART IV

	POUNDS		NEWTONS
13.	1	=	4.5 (N)
14.	10	=	_____ (N)
15.	100	=	_____ (_)
16.	150	=	_____ (_)
17.	200	=	_____ (_)

Complete the following using your weight.

18. My weight is (a)_____ lbs.

This equals (b)_____ grams or (c)_____ kilograms.

I weigh (d) _____ dynes or (e)_____ newtons (N).

COMPARING MEASUREMENTS OF WEIGHT

In the English system of measurement, weight is measured in pounds. In the metric system of measurement, weight is measured in newtons (N). An object with a mass of one kilogram (2.2 pounds) is pulled toward the center of the earth with a force of 9.8 newtons. The weight of the object in the metric system is 9.8 N.

Complete the following activity.

1. One kilogram equals _____ pounds.

2. One kilogram equals _____ newtons.

3. Two kilograms equal _____ pounds.

4. Two kilograms equal _____ newtons.

5. Five kilograms equal _____ pounds.

6. Five kilograms equal _____ newtons.

7. Ten kilograms equal _____ pounds.

8. Ten kilograms equal _____ newtons.

9. One hundred kilograms equal _____ newtons.

10. One hundred kilograms equal _____ pounds.

11. In the metric system, mass is measured in_____ or _____.

12. In the metric system, weight is measured in _____ or _____.

Name _____ Date _____

REVIEWING THE PROPERTIES OF MATTER

Use the words below to fill in the blanks in the following selection.

weight   mass   gravitational attraction   gravity   matter   force

All objects are made of (1) _____ . The amount of matter in an object determines the (2) _____ . All matter has (3) _____ and (4) _____ . The (5) _____ of an object remains constant. The (6) _____ of an object depends on how far an object is from the center of the earth. The weight of an object is determined by (7) _____ . The greater the mass of an object, the greater the (8) _____ _____ . Gravitational attraction is really a (9) _____ that pulls an object toward the center of the earth. This force is registered as the weight of an object.

10. Complete the following diagram. Fill in the rectangles with the following terms and statements.

matter   mass   weight   determined by gravity

gravity does not change   location determines amount

```
                    ┌──────────────────────┐
                    │(a)                   │
                    └──────────────────────┘
                      │                  │
                      ▼                  ▼
          ┌───────────────┐   ┌─────────────────┐
          │(b)            │   │(c)              │
          └───────────────┘   └─────────────────┘
                │                     │
                ▼                     ▼
  ┌─────────────────────┐   ┌─────────────────────────┐
  │(d)                  │   │(e)                      │
  └─────────────────────┘   └─────────────────────────┘
                                      │
                                      ▼
                            ┌─────────────────────────┐
                            │(f)                      │
                            └─────────────────────────┘
```

What Do You Think?

11. An object weighing 10 pounds is on a cliff. It is pushed off the cliff and is falling to the earth's surface at the base of the cliff. Why will the object not weigh 10 pounds while it is falling?

_____

_____

12. When an object is placed in water, it appears to weigh less. Why?

_____

_____

Name _____ Date _____

Understanding How Numbers Are Written in Science

When working with numbers in science that relate to mass and gravitation, it is often necessary to work with large numbers. Numbers may be written in **standard form**. For example, the number five thousand three hundred twenty in standard form is 5,320.

1. Write each of the following in standard form.

(a) Two hundred ten _____

(b) Six thousand four hundred twenty _____

(c) Ninety-six thousand five hundred forty _____

(d) One million six hundred thousand four hundred ten _____

(e) Three million five hundred thousand eight hundred _____

However, it is more common for very large numbers to be written in **scientific notation**.

Example: Numbers may be written as a power of ten.
             1,000 or $10*10*10 = 10^3$ in the form power of ten.

2. Complete the following table by changing each number to a power of ten.

	Number	Power of Ten
(a)	10	10^1
(b)	100	_____
(c)	1,000	10^3
(d)	10,000	_____
(e)	100,000	_____
(f)	1,000,000	_____

When numbers get extremely large or small like those used in science, it is easier to write numbers using scientific notation. Numbers are written in scientific notation form as **$a*10^x$**, using the numbers 1 through 10. In the form **$a*10^x$**, the letter "a" may be represented by any number, 1 through 10. For example, 1.0, 1.5, 3.45, 9.789, etc. The letter "x" may be any integer.

Example: $1*10^1$ is written in scientific notation. $1*10^{-1}$ is also written in scientific notation. In the examples, the number 1 could be replaced with any number from +1 through +10. The letter "x" could be any of the integers …-3, 0, +3….

Name _____ Date _____

HOW TO WRITE IN SCIENTIFIC NOTATION

Write the number 89,000,000 in scientific notation, in the form **a*10ˣ**:

Step 1:   Place a decimal point between the 8 and 9 and write as 8.9. This gives a number that is between +1 and +10.

Step 2:   Start on the right and count the number of decimal places to the decimal point. There are seven. 8.<u>9,000,000</u>.

Step 3:   Write 89,000,000 in scientific notation. $8.9*10^7$

Step 4:   Check to see that the number 89,000,000 is written in the form **a*10ˣ**:
"a" = 8.9, which is between the numbers +1 and +10
* = multiplication sign following 8.9, which replaced the letter "a"
$10^x = 10^7$, which is written to represent 10*10*10*10*10*10*10
$8.9*10^7 = 8.9*10,000,000 = 89,000,000$

The numbers below represent the distance of the earth and other planets from the Sun. The numbers are in miles. Write each number in scientific notation.

1. Mercury: 36,000,000 _____
2. Venus: 66,900,000 _____
3. Earth: 93,000,000 _____
4. Mars: 141,000,000 _____

The numbers below represent the diameters of some of the planets in meters. Write each number in scientific notation.

5. Earth: 12,800,000 _____
6. Jupiter: 120,500,000 _____
7. Saturn: 119,800,000 _____
8. Uranus: 51,100,000 _____
9. Neptune: 49,500,000 _____
10. Pluto: 2,340,000 _____

Name _____ Date _____

Understanding Mass and Gravity

There are two very important factors that affect gravitational force.
1. The larger the mass of an object, the greater the gravitational force.
2. The closer objects are, the greater the gravitational force.

Answer the following questions.

1. An individual was weighed on Earth before flying to various altitudes. The scale registered 150 pounds on Earth. Place a plus (+) beside the statements below that are true. Place a minus (-) beside the statements that are false. On the blank below each statement, write why the statement is true or false.

_____ (a) The same individual in a plane flying at an altitude of 30,000 feet will weigh less than 150 pounds.

_____

_____ (b) The mass of the individual at 30,000 feet is different than the mass of the individual on the earth's surface.

_____

_____ (c) The weight of the individual on the surface of the earth and at 30,000 feet will be 150 pounds.

_____

_____ (d) The weight of the individual will be less at 40,000 feet than at 30,000 feet.

_____

_____ (e) The masses of the individual and the earth will not change.

_____

Circle the correct choices:

2. A man weighs 180 pounds. He walks up a mountain to an elevation of 15,000 feet. His weight at 15,000 feet will:

(a) (increase/decrease) because he is moving

(b) (away from/toward) the earth's center.

The man (c) (will/will not) lose matter as he reaches the 15,000-foot elevation.

Name _____ Date _____

Understanding Mass and Gravity (continued)

3. The diagram below represents a female astronaut on the surface of the earth at point "a". The astronaut is part of a crew that will fly a space mission on a given day. Below are five numbers that represent the weight of the female astronaut on the day of the given space mission. Place the numbers in order in the appropriate rectangles to represent the changing weight of the astronaut as the flight leaves Earth.

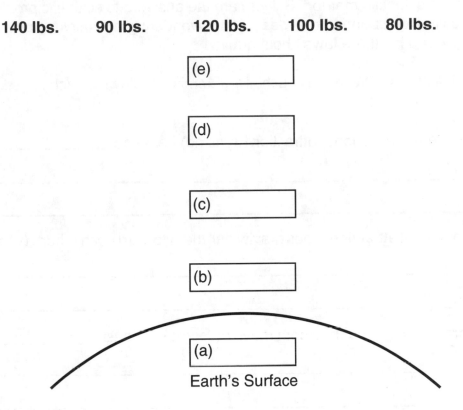

140 lbs.   90 lbs.   120 lbs.   100 lbs.   80 lbs.

(e)

(d)

(c)

(b)

(a)

Earth's Surface

Circle the correct choices:

4. A rectangular piece of iron weighs 96 pounds on the surface of the earth. The piece of iron is transported to the moon and weighed. The weight of the rectangular piece of iron on the moon's surface is 16 pounds.

    (a) The mass of the moon is (more/less) than the earth.

    (b) The force of gravity is (less/more) than on Earth.

    (c) The mass of the iron on the moon is (different than/the same as) on Earth.

    (d) The weight of the iron on the moon is (a) 1/4   (b) 1/2   (c) 1/6   (d) 1/10   of the weight on earth.

    (e) The gravitational force on the moon is (a) 1/4   (b) 1/2   (c) 1/6   (d) 1/10   of the gravitational force on earth.

    (f) Gravitational force and weight (are/are not) related.

Name _____ Date _____

QUESTIONS ABOUT GRAVITY

  Sir Isaac Newton developed the **law of gravitation**. According to Newton's law, every object in the universe attracts every other object. He called the force of attraction between objects **gravitational attraction**. The amount of gravitational attraction between objects depends on how much **mass** the objects have and how **far apart** the objects are.

  In the study of science, it is important to ask questions. Trying out various possibilities for answers is part of the scientific method. Seldom are the answers to scientific problems found on the first trial. Isaac Newton spent a great deal of time wondering and thinking about why objects fall before he developed his three laws about gravity.

The exercise that follows is a "What do you think?" exercise. Following each question, write what you think the answer might be.

1. Do all objects have a gravitational attraction? (yes/no) because _____

_____

_____

2. If objects have a mutual attraction, does gravity pull them toward each other? (yes/no) because

_____

_____

3. If two objects are attracted, do they both move? (yes/no) because _____

_____

_____

4. When a rock is thrown off a cliff, does the rock fall to earth? (yes/no) because _____

_____

_____

5. Does the earth move toward the rock? (yes/no) because _____

_____

_____

6. Does a tennis ball fall faster than a baseball? (yes/no) because _____

_____

_____

Name _____ Date _____

HOW GRAVITY AND TIME AFFECT THE DISTANCE AND SPEED OF A FALLING OBJECT

Gravity affects the distance an object will fall in a given period of time. Gravity also affects the speed of an object as the period of time passes.

An important formula for finding the distance an object will fall in a given amount of time is **d = 16t²**. This formula says that **distance** equals 16 multiplied by **time squared**. The letter "d" in the formula stands for distance. The letter "t" stands for time.

To square "t" (time) means that the number substituted in the formula for "t" is multiplied times itself. If "t" equals 2, then "t²" equals 2*2 or 4.

In the following exercises, find the square for each problem.

1. When "t" equals 2, then t^2 equals 2^2 or 2*2 = 4.

2. When "t" equals 3, then t^2 equals 3^2 or ____ * ____ = _____.

3. When "t" equals 4, then t^2 equals ____ ^{2} or ____ * ____ = _____.

4. When "t" equals 1, then t^2 equals ____ ^{2} or ____ * ____ = _____.

5. When "t" equals 5, then t^2 equals ____ ^{2} or ____ * ____ = _____.

6. When "t" equals 6, then t^2 equals ____ ^{2} or ____ * ____ = _____.

When using the formula to determine the distance an object falls, **time** is measured from the **instant** the object is dropped. **Distance** is measured downward from the **point** where the object is dropped.

Chart I below shows the distance a ball falls when dropped from the roof of a 400-foot building. The chart shows the time and the formula for determining the distance the ball falls each second.

CHART I

Time Ball Falls	Formula			Distance Ball Falls
1 second	$d = 16t^2$	so	$16 = 16*1^2$	16
2 seconds	$d = 16t^2$	so	$16 = 16*2^2$	64
3 seconds	$d = 16t^2$	so	$16 = 16*3^2$	144
4 seconds	$d = 16t^2$	so	$16 = 16*4^2$	256
5 seconds	$d = 16t^2$	so	$16 = 16*5^2$	400

Name _____ Date _____

How Gravity and Time Affect the Distance and Speed of a Falling Object (continued)

Refer to Chart I and answer the following:

7. In _____ seconds, the ball falls 16 feet.

8. In 3 seconds, the ball falls _____ feet.

9. In 5 seconds, the ball falls _____ feet.

10. Two hundred fifty-six feet is the distance the ball falls in _____ seconds.

11. In the formula **d = 16t²** in Chart I, one element of the formula never changes when solving a problem. That element is the number _____ . In working with formulas, you will often find there is an element that always represents the same number. The number in a formula that is always the same is called the **constant**.

12. Each of the squares on the line below equals 16 feet. Show the distance the ball in Chart I falls each second. Place numbers in the square(s) to show the distance the ball falls for each second.
1 = one second, 2 = two seconds, 3 = three seconds, 4 = four seconds, 5 = five seconds

<table>
<tr><td></td><td></td><td></td><td></td><td></td><td></td><td></td><td></td><td></td><td></td><td></td><td></td><td></td><td></td><td></td><td></td><td></td><td></td><td></td><td></td><td></td><td></td><td></td><td></td><td></td><td></td><td></td><td></td><td></td><td></td><td></td><td></td><td></td></tr>
</table>

Answer the following. Complete all steps.

Step 1	Step 2	Step 3	Step 4
13. d = 16t²	d = 16*1²	d = 16 * 1	d = 16
14. d = 16t²	d = 16*2²	d = ____ * ____	d = ____
15. d = 16t²	d = 16*3²	d = ____ * ____	d = ____
16. d = 16t²	d = 16*4²	d = ____ * ____	d = ____
17. d = 16t²	d = 16*5²	d = ____ * ____	d = ____

Name _____ Date _____

USING THE METRIC SYSTEM IN DISTANCE AND SPEED PROBLEMS

When solving problems in science, two systems of measurement are used. One is the **English system**, which is common in the United States. In many other nations, the **metric system** is used. Chart II below is in meters.

Complete Chart II using meters rather than feet. To convert **d = 16t² feet** to meters, the 16 feet must be changed to meters. One meter equals 3.28 feet. Sixteen divided by 3.28 equals 4.9 meters. The formula for the distance in meters a ball will fall each second when dropped from the building in Chart II becomes **d = 4.9t²**. The first one has been completed for you.

CHART II

	Step 1	Step 2	Step 3	Step 4
1.	$d = 4.9t^2$	$d = 4.9*1^2$	$d = 4.9 * 1$	$d = 4.9$
2.	$d = 4.9t^2$	$d = 4.9*2^2$	___ = ___ * ____	$d =$ _____
3.	$d = 4.9t^2$	$d = 4.9*3^2$	___ = ___ * ____	$d =$ _____
4.	$d = 4.9t^2$	$d = 4.9*4^2$	___ = ___ * ____	$d =$ _____
5.	$d = 4.9t^2$	$d = 4.9*5^2$	___ = ___ * ____	$d =$ _____

Convert each of the following from feet to meters. To convert feet to meters, divide the feet by 3.28. Round answers to the nearest whole number.

6. 16 feet = _____ meters

7. 32 feet = _____ meters

8. 48 feet = _____ meters

9. 96 feet = _____ meters

To convert meters to feet, multiply 3.28 (the number of feet in a meter) times the meters to be converted. Convert 4.9 meters to feet. 4.9*3.28 = 16.07 or 16 feet.

Convert each of the following from meters to feet. Round answers to the nearest whole number.

10. 19.6 meters = _____ feet

11. 39.2 meters = _____ feet

12. 176.4 meters = _____ feet

13. 240.1 meters = _____ feet

14. 88.2 meters = _____ feet

15. 98 meters = _____ feet

Name _____ Date _____

HOW GRAVITY AND TIME AFFECT THE SPEED OF A FALLING OBJECT

The force that gravity exerts on a falling object causes the object to **accelerate** (gain speed) as it falls. When an object is dropped from a building, the **initial** (beginning) acceleration is zero. The object gains speed (accelerates) at the rate of 32 feet per second.

So speed (acceleration) equals 32 multiplied by time. The formula for the speed of a falling object then becomes **speed = 32t** or **s = 32t**.

Example: An object falls for two seconds.

Step 1	**Step 2**	**Step 3**
Speed = 32*t	Speed = 32 (feet)*2 (seconds)	Speed = 64 feet per second

Complete the following to find the speed in feet of a baseball dropped from a building. Show your work below each question. Use the formula to find the correct answer.

1. The ball's speed after two seconds is _____ feet per second.

2. The ball's speed after five seconds is _____ per second.

3. The ball's speed after eight seconds is _____.

Refer back to Chart I on page 13 to solve the following.

4. The distance the ball falls in feet after two seconds is _____ feet.
5. The distance the ball falls in feet after five seconds is _____ feet.
6. The distance the ball falls in feet after eight seconds is _____ feet.

Name _____ Date _____

HOW GRAVITY AND TIME AFFECT THE SPEED OF A FALLING OBJECT
(CONTINUED)

In determining the **acceleration rate** or speed of a falling object, meters per second are often used rather than feet per second. A meter equals 3.28 feet. To determine the number of meters to use in place of 32 feet, divide 32 by 3.28.

Thirty-two divided by 3.28 = 32/3.28 = 9.8 meters. The formula for the speed of a dropped ball in meters becomes **speed = 9.8t** or **s = 9.8t**.

Complete the following to find the speed in meters of a baseball dropped from a building. Show your work below each question. Use the formula to find the correct answer.

7. The ball's speed after two seconds is _____ meters per second.

8. The ball's speed after five seconds is _____ per second.

9. The ball's speed after eight seconds is _____.

Refer back to Chart II on page 15 to answer the following.

10. The distance the ball falls in meters after two seconds is _____ meters.

11. The distance the ball falls in meters after five seconds is _____ meters.

12. The distance the ball falls in meters after eight seconds is _____ meters.

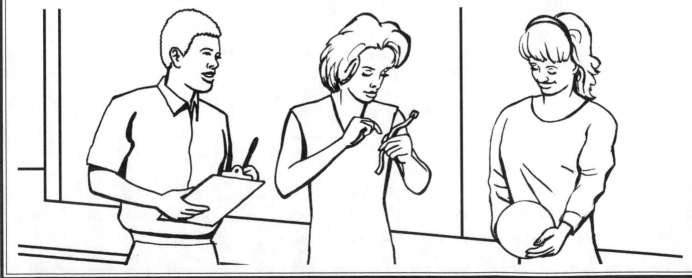

Name _____ Date _____

REVIEWING GRAVITY, TIME, DISTANCE, AND SPEED

What Do You Think?

Emily, Stephany, and Megan are on the roof of the building in Chart I. Emily drops a baseball from the roof. At the same time, Stephany throws a baseball downward from the roof with a speed of 64 feet per second. Megan throws a baseball from the roof horizontally with a speed of 64 feet per second.

1. Which ball will hit the ground first? _____

2. Which ball will reach the greatest speed? _____

3. Write Emily, Stephany, and Megan under the diagram below that shows the path each ball will travel when falling. In the space below the diagram, explain your answer.

(a)_____   (b) _____   (c) _____

_____

_____

_____

Chart III below shows the distance the ball thrown downward by Stephany will fall each second. Refer to Chart I on page 13 and Chart III to answer the questions that follow.

CHART III

Time Ball Falls	Distance Ball Falls (feet)
1 second	80
2 seconds	128
3 seconds	208
4 seconds	(11) _____
5 seconds	(12) _____

4. In Chart I, the distance the ball falls after one second is _____ feet.

5. In Chart III, the distance the ball falls after one second is _____ feet greater than in Chart I.

6. In Chart I, the distance the ball falls after two seconds is _____ feet.

Name _____ _____ Date _____

REVIEWING GRAVITY, TIME, DISTANCE, AND SPEED (CONTINUED)

7. In Chart III, the distance a ball falls after two seconds is _____ feet greater than in Chart I.

8. In Chart I, the distance the ball falls after three seconds is _____ feet.

9. In Chart III, the distance the ball falls after three seconds is _____ feet greater than in Chart I.

10. The distance the ball falls in **Chart III** for each second is _____ feet **greater** than in **Chart I**.

11. Write the distance the ball falls in four seconds on the blank in Chart III.

12. Write the distance the ball falls in five seconds on the blank in Chart III.

Each of the squares in A and B below equals 16 feet. Use the colors red (one second), blue (two seconds), yellow (three seconds), orange (four seconds), and black (five seconds). Refer to Chart I and color in the squares in A that represent the distance in feet the ball falls each second. Refer to Chart III and color in the squares in B that represent the distance the ball falls in feet each second. Each rectangle in C equals 4.9 meters. Refer to Chart II and color in the squares in C that represent the distance in meters the ball falls each second.

What about the ball thrown horizontally by Megan? What path will the ball travel? Refer to Chart IV below and complete the following.

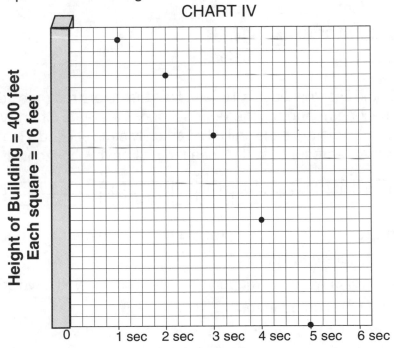

CHART IV

Height of Building = 400 feet
Each square = 16 feet

0   1 sec   2 sec   3 sec   4 sec   5 sec   6 sec

Horizontal Distance Ball Travels Each Second
Each square = 16 feet

13. Connect the dots on Chart IV with a line to show the path of the baseball thrown by Megan.

14. Each of the squares on the graph equals _____ feet.

Name _____ Date _____

REVIEWING GRAVITY, TIME, DISTANCE, AND SPEED (CONTINUED)

15. The left side of Chart IV shows the building from which Megan is throwing the ball in a horizontal direction. The vertical line of the graph measures (a) the distance of the ball from the building each second (b) the distance the ball falls each second. (circle one)

16. The horizontal line at the bottom of the graph measures (a) the distance of the ball from the building each second (b) the distance the ball falls each second. (circle one)

Fill in the blanks that show the distance the ball is from the building after each second.

Distance Ball Is From Building

17. 1 second   _____ feet or _____ meters

18. 2 seconds   _____ feet or _____ meters

19. 3 seconds   _____ feet or _____ meters

20. 4 seconds   _____ feet or _____ meters

Fill in the blanks that show the distance the ball falls after each second.

Distance Ball Falls

21. 1 second   _____ feet or _____ meters

22. 2 seconds   _____ feet or _____ meters

23. 3 seconds   _____ feet or _____ meters

24. 4 seconds   _____ feet or _____ meters

Each of the squares in D and E below equals 16 feet. Use the colors red (one second), blue (two seconds), yellow (three seconds), and orange (four seconds). Refer to Chart IV and color in the squares in D that represent the distance the ball falls vertically each second. Refer to Chart IV and color in the squares in E that represent the distance the ball travels horizontally each second.

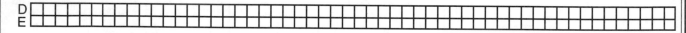

25. In "D" above, the formula   (a) d = 16*t   (b) d = 64*t²   (c) d = 64*t   (d) d = 16*t² shows the distance the balls falls each second.

26. On the back of this sheet or on your own paper, prove the formula you have chosen by working two problems using the data presented in row "D".

27. In "E" above, the formula   (a) d = 16*t²   (b) d = 64*t   (c) d = 64*t²   (d) d = 16*t shows the distance the ball travels horizontally each second.

28. On the back of this sheet or on your own paper, prove the formula you have chosen by working two problems using the data presented in row "E".

Name _____ Date _____

DRAWING A PARABOLA

What Do You Think?

Emily, Stephany, and Megan are trying out for the softball team. The coach tells them that one of them will be chosen to start in the next game in the center-field position. The coach, who is also their physical science teacher, tells them they are equal in hitting and fielding skills. The one chosen to start will be the one who demonstrates the best ability to throw the ball from center field to home plate. The coach tells them an outfielder must have a good throwing arm and understand how a parabola affects the flight of the ball.

In the space below, draw a diagram of a parabola. Then explain what you think a parabola is and why it is important in throwing the ball from the outfield to home plate.

1. Draw a parabola.

2. Explain how the parabola affects throwing the ball. _____

_____

_____

3. A football player standing on the 10-yard line throws a pass to a receiver on the 50-yard line. Select from a, b, and c below the path of the football from the player on the 10-yard line to the player on the 50-yard line. (Circle the letter of the correct path.)

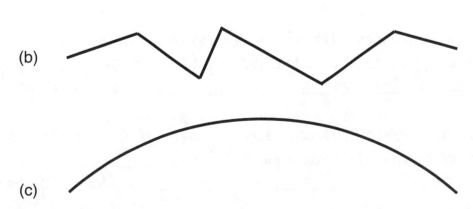

(a)

(b)

(c)

4. The flight path of the football in Question 3 is a _____.

21

Name _____ Date _____

PLOTTING A PARABOLA

When a baseball or football is thrown, the path of the ball often forms a **parabola**. To plot the path of a parabola or the path of a football or baseball, it is important to first determine how many seconds the ball will rise before beginning to fall. Once this is determined, it is then possible to plot the parabola.

A baseball is thrown upward with a velocity of 96 feet per second.
How long will it take for the baseball to reach its maximum height and begin to fall back to earth?

Think: Gravity will begin to pull the ball back to earth as soon as it is thrown. After each second, the ball will be falling back to earth at the speed of 32 feet per second. Remember **32*t**.

Think: Find how many seconds it will take for the pull of gravity to overcome the beginning speed of 96 feet per second.

Think: 96 divided by 32 equals 3. So 3*32 = 96. In three seconds, the pull of gravity will have equaled the beginning speed of 96 feet per second.

Think: 96 - 96 = 0. So in three seconds, the speed of the baseball will be zero. It will now begin to fall back to earth.

The formula for determining the number of seconds it will take the baseball thrown upward at a speed of 96 feet per second to reach its maximum height is: **speed (0) = 96 - 32t**
$$\text{speed} = 96 - 32t = 96 - 32*3 = 96 - 96 = 0$$
In three seconds, the speed of the baseball is zero, and the ball begins to fall back to earth.

Complete the following. Use the formula.

1. A ball is thrown upward with a speed of 64 feet per second. How many seconds until the speed of the ball is zero and the ball begins to fall back to earth?   (a) 0 = 64 - 32t
(b) 64/32 = _____ (c) 0 = 64 - 32* _____   (d) In _____ seconds, the ball will begin to fall back to earth.

2. A ball is thrown upward with a speed of 128 feet per second. How many seconds until the speed of the ball is zero and the ball begins to fall back to earth?   (a) 0 = 128 - 32t
(b) _____ /32 = ____   (c) 0 = _____ - 32* _____   d) In _____ seconds, the ball will begin to fall back to earth.

3. A ball is thrown upward with a speed of 320 feet per second. How many seconds until the speed of the ball is zero and the ball begins to fall back to earth?   (a) 0 = _____ - _____t
(b) _____ / ____ = _____   (c) 0 = _____ - ____ * _____   (d) In _____ seconds, the ball will begin to fall back to earth.

Name _____ Date _____

LEARNING HOW HIGH THE OBJECT WILL BE AFTER EACH SECOND

In the exercise on page 22, you have determined the time it takes for an object thrown upward to reach a speed of zero and begin to fall back to earth. When an object is thrown into space, it is often important to know how high the object is at various times. The graph below shows the flight of a baseball thrown upward with a speed of 96 feet per second. The formula **d = 96*t - 16*t²** was used to plot the height of the ball for each second the ball was in flight. Refer to the graph and answer the following questions.

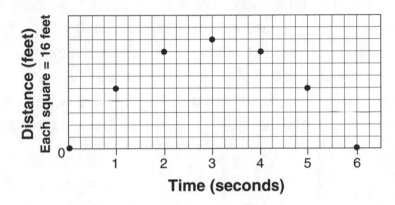

1. Begin at zero and draw a line connecting the dots and extending down to the base line at the six-second mark.

2. The shape of the line drawn is a _____ .

3. The height of the ball at one second is _____ feet.

4. The height of the ball at two seconds is _____ feet.

5. The height of the ball at three seconds is _____ feet.

6. The height of the ball at four seconds is _____ feet.

7. The height of the ball at five seconds is _____ feet.

8. The ball is at its highest point at _____ seconds.

9. The ball reaches zero speed at _____ seconds and begins to fall back to earth.

10. In the space below, draw the flight of the ball for the period zero through two seconds and four seconds through six seconds. On the lines below the drawing, write what you found.

_____

_____

_____

Name _____ Date _____

MORE PARABOLA PRACTICE

In #1 and #2 below, determine the time it will take for the object to reach its highest point. Then determine the distance the object is above the earth for each second. Plot the flights of the objects for each second on the graph below by using the formula $d = 128t - 16t^2$ or $d = 39.2t - 4.9t^2$ for each second from 0 to the highest point. Since the flight is a parabola, the distances for the descent will correspond to those of the ascent.

1. An object is thrown upward with the speed of 128 feet per second.

    a) Time to reach highest point _____ seconds. Use the formula $0 = 128 - 32t$.

    b) Distance above the earth at highest point is _____ feet. Use the formula $d = 128t - 16t^2$.

2. An object is thrown upward with a speed of 39.2 meters per second.

    a) Time to reach highest point _____ seconds. Use the formula $0 = 39.2 - 9.8t$.

    b) Distance above the earth at highest point is _____ meters. Use the formula $d = 39.2t - 4.9t^2$.

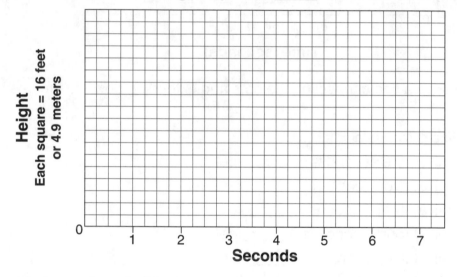

Height Each square = 16 feet or 4.9 meters

Seconds

3. In Figure 1 below, a baseball is dropped from Point A. At the same time, a baseball is thrown from Point B. Which one will hit the ground first? _____ Why? _____
_____

4. In Figure 2 below, a baseball is thrown from Point A across the building to Point B. The distance from Point A to the nearest corner of the building is 50 feet. What is the distance from the nearest corner of the building to Point B where the baseball landed? _____
Why? _____

5. In Figure 2 below, what is the shape of the ball's path from Point A to Point B? _____

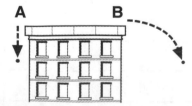

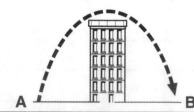

Name _____ Date _____

REVIEWING WHAT HAS BEEN LEARNED

Match each term in Column A with the correct meaning in Column B.

Column A	Column B
____ 1. Gravity	A. Mathematical figure showing path of ball thrown from Point A to B
____ 2. Velocity	B. Causes friction as an object falls through the air
____ 3. Accelerated motion	C. Causes objects to fall to Earth
____ 4. Resistance of air	D. Tells how fast an object is falling
____ 5. Terminal velocity	E. Refers to the speed and direction an object is moving
____ 6. Projectile	F. Refers to the increasing speed as an object falls
____ 7. Parabola	G. A bullet is an example.
____ 8. Speed	H. Velocity reached when the velocity of a falling object will not continue to increase.

REVIEWING THE EFFECTS OF GRAVITY

1. In the space below, explain how you think the flight of a baseball thrown upward with a speed of 64 feet per second would be affected if gravity on Earth were doubled.

_____

_____

_____

When an object is thrown upward with a certain speed, it is important to find how long it will be before the speed of the object reaches zero and the object begins to fall back to Earth. When an object is thrown upward, the force of gravity immediately begins to pull the object back toward Earth. If there were no gravity, the object would continue its flight and never return to the earth's surface. The gravitational pull of the earth causes an object to fall toward the earth at the speed of 32 feet per second. So, if one knows the speed at which an object is thrown upward, a formula can be used to determine when the speed of the object will be zero and the object will begin falling back toward Earth.

Example: A ball is thrown upward at a speed of 96 feet per second. Immediately, the force of gravity begins to pull the ball back toward the earth at a speed of 32 fet per second.

The formula **0 = 96 - 32t** can be used to determine when the upward speed of the ball will reach zero. (The 96 in the formula is changed if the upward speed of the ball is a different speed.)

After one second, the ball's speed = 96 - 32*1 = 64 feet per second.

After two seconds, the ball's speed equals 96 - 32*2 = 32 feet per second.

After three seconds, the ball's speed equals 96 - 32*3 = 0 feet per second. The ball reaches its greatest height and begins to fall back to Earth.

Name _____ Date _____

REVIEWING THE EFFECTS OF GRAVITY (CONTINUED)

When an object is thrown upward, it is important to know what the height will be when the speed of the object reaches zero. Another formula can be used to find the height of the ball when the speed is at zero. The formula for the height of the object is **height = 96t -16t²**. In the example, the formula would be 96*3 - 16*3² = 144 feet. The three in the formula represents the second when the speed is zero. The number for "t" is always the amount of time for the object to reach a speed of zero.

2. Determine the time it takes for a ball thrown upward with a speed of 96 feet per second to reach zero speed if the force of gravity were 16 feet per second rather than 32. Use the formula 0 = 96-16t.

Complete the formula for the first second, and then repeat the process on your own paper or the back of this sheet until you have determined the time it takes the speed to reach zero.

(a) After one second, the ball's speed equals _____ - _____ * _____ = _____ feet per second.

(b) The ball will reach the speed of zero at the end of _____ seconds.

(c) Fill in the following formula to find the height of the ball when the speed is zero. The letter "t" should be replaced with the second when the speed of the ball reaches zero.

   96t - 8t² = 96 * ___ - 8 * ___ ² = _____ feet

3. Determine the time it takes for a ball thrown upward with a speed of 96 feet per second to reach zero speed if the force of gravity were 8 feet per second rather than 32. Use the formula 0 = 96-8t.

Complete the formula for the first second, and then repeat the process on your own paper or the back of this sheet until you have determined the time it takes the speed to reach zero.

(a) After one second, the ball's speed equals _____ - _____ * _____ = _____ feet per second.

(b) The ball will reach the speed of zero at the end of _____ seconds.

(c) Fill in the following formula to find the height of the ball when the speed is zero. The letter "t" should be replaced with the second when the speed of the ball reaches zero.

   96t - 4t² = 96 * _____ - 4 * ___ ² = _____ feet

4. The force of gravity in Question 3 is   (a)$\frac{1}{2}$ (b) 2 times   (c)$\frac{1}{4}$ (d) $\frac{1}{10}$ the force of gravity in Question 2.

5. The time for the ball to reach a speed of zero in Question 3 is   (a)$\frac{1}{2}$ (b) 2 times   (c)$\frac{1}{4}$ (d) $\frac{1}{10}$ the time in Question 2.

6. Write the simple fraction that represents the height of the ball in Question 2 compared with the height in Question 3. _____

Name _____ Date _____

Understanding Motion

Motion is something that is part of your everyday life. **Motion refers to bodies moving.** Automobiles, the earth, people, and many other things are in motion.

To understand motion, the meaning of the terms **speed, velocity,** and **acceleration** must be understood.

Speed is the distance traveled by a moving object in a given time. To determine speed, the distance traveled is divided by time.

The formula is **speed** = $\dfrac{\textbf{distance}}{\textbf{time}}$

An automobile trip is 400 miles. The time to travel the 400 miles is 10 hours.

Speed = $\dfrac{400}{10}$ = 40 miles per hour.

Solve the following.

1. Find the speed of a long-distance runner who runs 30 miles in 6 hours. _____

2. A jet airplane flies from St. Louis, Missouri, to Phoenix, Arizona, in 3 hours. The distance is 1,500 miles. The speed is _____ per _____.

3. It takes a runner 10 seconds to run 100 yards. The runner's speed is _____ per _____.

4. A sprinter runs the 100-meter race in 10 seconds. The sprinter's speed is_____ per _____.

5. A train travels a distance of 1,200 kilometers in 20 hours. The speed is _____ per _____.

Velocity is speed in a specific direction. A car that travels 500 miles in 10 hours is traveling at a speed of 50 miles per hour toward the southeast. The speed of the car is 50 miles per hour. The velocity of the car is 50 miles per hour/southeast.

6. Find the velocity of a long-distance runner who runs south for 30 miles in 6 hours. _____ per hour/ _____.

7. A jet airplane flies southwest from St. Louis, Missouri, to Phoenix, Arizona, in 3 hours. The distance is 1,500 miles. The velocity is _____ per hour/ _____.

8. A train travels north a distance of 1,200 kilometers in 20 hours. The velocity is _____ per hour/ _____.

Name _____ Date _____

Understanding Motion (continued)

Acceleration is the rate of change in velocity. A car is traveling southeast at 50 miles per hour for two hours. Then the car speeds up for three hours to a speed of 70 miles per hour. The velocity of the car was 50 miles per hour/southeast for two hours. Then the velocity changed from 50 to 70 miles per hour/southeast for three hours. When the car's velocity changed from 50 to 70 miles per hour, it **accelerated**.

The formula for finding acceleration is: $$\text{acceleration} = \frac{\text{final velocity - initial velocity}}{\text{time}}$$

final velocity = ending velocity   initial velocity = beginning velocity

9. Find the acceleration of a long-distance runner at a velocity of 5 miles per hour/west. In the next 2 hours, he increases his velocity to 7 miles per hour/west. His rate of acceleration is _____ mph per hour.

10. A jet is flying at a velocity of 500 kilometers per hour/east. In the next 4 hours, the pilot increases the velocity to 700 kilometers per hour/east. The rate of acceleration is _____ kph per hour.

11. A jet is flying at a velocity of 700 kilometers per hour/southwest. In the next 4 hours, the pilot **decelerates** the velocity to 500 kilometers per hour/southwest. The rate of deceleration is _____ kph per hour.

12. A 5,000-meter runner runs the first 1,000 meters at a velocity of 5.5 meters per second/west. In sixty seconds, she increases her velocity and is running 1,000 meters at a velocity of 7 meters per second/west. The rate of acceleration is _____ meters per second per _____.

Name _____ Date _____

MORE MOTION NOTIONS

The following terms are all important in understanding motion. Read the passage below and fill in the blanks with the terms. Some terms may be used more than once.

accelerating   average   centripetal   accelerated   speed
decelerated   momentum   decelerate   velocity

Emily settled into her new Camaro and adjusted her seat belt. She knew the trip would take most of the day. However, if all went well, she would have traveled 390 miles before stopping for the night.

Slowly Emily moved onto the highway, (1)_____ until she reached a speed of 65 miles per hour. Checking the speedometer, she set the odometer at zero. She thought if she could maintain an (2)_____ speed of 65 miles per hour, the trip would take six hours.

After driving for three hours, she began to feel the pangs of hunger. She saw a road sign advertising sandwiches and decided to stop. She (3)_____ to a speed of 35 and then totally lost all (4)_____ as the car stopped.

Back on the highway, she thought about how much she had enjoyed the sandwich and the one-hour break from driving. She pushed down on the accelerator and (5)_____ until the speedometer registered 65 miles per hour. She maintained the speed until she came to a curve and had to (6)_____ to a speed of 60. She thought that when traveling around a curve, (7)_____ acceleration makes it much like a rocket ship traveling around the earth.

Once around the curve, she came up on a car traveling a little slower than her speed. She (8)_____ to 70 and passed the other car. Once she was safely back in the right lane, she (9)_____ back to the original speed of 65.

Pulling in at the hotel, she noted on the odometer that she had traveled 390 miles. Checking her watch, Emily noted that it was 7 hours since she began the trip. She divided 390 by 7 and determined that the (10)_____ speed had been 56 miles per hour. Suddenly she remembered she had stopped an hour for lunch. She then divided 390 by 6 and found that the correct average (11)_____ was 65 miles per hour.

Name _____ Date _____

LEARNING MORE ABOUT ACCELERATION AND DECELERATION

acceleration (a) = $\dfrac{\text{terminal speed } (s_2) \; - \; \text{initial speed } (s_1)}{\text{time } (t)}$

Complete the following:

The formula for rate of acceleration is: $a = \dfrac{s_2 - s_1}{t}$

1. a = _____

2. s_2 = _____

3. s_1 = _____

Fill in each blank using one of the following terms.

change   **beginning**   **ending**

4. The initial speed means the _____ speed.

5. The terminal speed means the _____ speed.

6. Acceleration means the _____ in speed.

   In solving acceleration problems, the English or metric measurement system may be used. If the English system is used, the speeds will be in miles per hour. If the metric system is used, the speeds will be in kilometers per hour.

In solving the following problems:

   One kilometer equals $\frac{6}{10}$ (0.6) of one mile.

   One and six-tenths kilometers ($1\frac{6}{10}$ or 1.6) equal one mile.

Complete the blanks by placing the numbers on the correct blanks to complete the formula.

a = 10 s_2 = 60 s_1 = 30   t = 3   (speeds in miles per hour [mph])

7. ____ = $\dfrac{\text{____} - \text{____}}{\text{____}}$

8. In the above formula, speed is in miles per hour. Time is in minutes. Acceleration is in miles per hour _____ minute.

9. The initial speed is 20 miles per hour. The terminal speed is 50 miles per hour. The time of acceleration from 20 miles per hour to 50 miles per hour is 3 minutes. Complete the formula and determine the acceleration rate.

a = ? s_2 = 50 s_1 = 20   t = 3

10. ____ = $\dfrac{\text{____} - \text{____}}{\text{____}}$

Name _____ Date _____

LEARNING MORE ABOUT ACCELERATION AND DECELERATION (CONT.)

11. Change the speeds in Problem #10 to kilometers per hour. (a) s_1 = _____ kilometers, (b) s_2 = _____ kilometers. Rewrite the formula in Problem #10 using kilometers for the speeds.

c) ____ = $\dfrac{\overline{\quad} - \overline{\quad}}{\overline{\quad}}$

Complete each of the following formulas and solve the equation.
Example:

      time = 5 min.   initial speed = 50 mph   terminal speed = 70 mph

$$a = \frac{s_2 - s_1}{t} = \frac{70 - 50}{5} = \frac{20}{5} = 4 \text{ mph per minute}$$

12. initial speed 0, terminal speed 88 feet per second, time 5 seconds

    The rate of acceleration is _____ per _____.

13. initial speed 0, terminal speed 60 feet per second, time 4 seconds

    The rate of acceleration is _____ per _____.

14. initial speed 40 feet per second, terminal speed 88 feet per second, time 5 seconds

    The rate of acceleration is _____ per _____.

15. initial speed 0 meters per second, terminal speed 30 meters per second, time 3 seconds

    The rate of acceleration is _____ per _____.

16. initial speed 88 feet per second, terminal speed 44 feet per second, time 4 seconds

    The rate of deceleration is _____ per _____. (drop the negative sign)

17. initial speed 30 meters per second, terminal speed 0 meters per second, time 2 seconds

    The rate of deceleration is _____ per _____. (drop the negative sign)

18. The speed of an automobile is 35 mph. The driver accelerates to 50 mph in 3 minutes. The acceleration is _____ per minute.

19. A car's speed is now 40 miles per hour. The driver has accelerated for 5 minutes at a rate of 3 mph per minute. The initial speed was _____ .

20. The speed of an automobile is 100 kilometers per hour. The driver decelerates slowly to a speed of 60 kilometers per hour. The deceleration time is 4 minutes.

    (a) The initial speed is_____ kilometers per _____ .

    (b) The terminal speed is _____ kilometers per _____.

    (c) The driver decelerates at a speed of _____ kph per _____.

    (d) The initial speed of the automobile in miles per hour is _____.

    (e) The terminal speed of the automobile in miles per hour is _____.

    (f) The deceleration rate in miles per hour is _____ per _____.

Name _____ Date _____

SPEED, VELOCITY, AND DISPLACEMENT

Speed and velocity are two terms that are frequently used when motion is discussed. However, they do not mean the same thing. Speed is used when referring to the **rate of motion**. Velocity refers to **rate of motion** and **displacement**.

Displacement refers to the **distance** and **direction** an object is from a fixed point. For example, an object is located 100 miles north of Chicago, Illinois. An automobile is located 80 meters southeast of Santa Fe, New Mexico.

Match each definition in Column B with the correct term in Column A.

Column A
_____ 1. Speed

_____ 2. Displacement

_____ 3. Velocity

Column B

a. refers to both the distance and direction of an object moving 50 kilometers per hour toward the northeast

b. refers only to the speed at which an object is moving (50 kilometers per hour)

c. refers to the distance and direction an object is from a specific point (50 kilometers northeast of Quincy, Illinois)

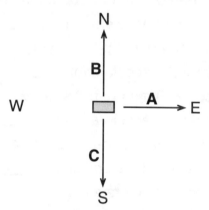

The diagram at right shows an automobile in the center of the diagram. The automobile may move in the direction of any one of the arrows labeled A, B, or C. The automobile will always move at an average speed of 50 mph. The time of travel is 2 hours. Answer each of the following questions. Answers will include one of the following directions: **south, north, east, west.**

4. Which direction will the automobile move if it travels on the route labeled A? _____

5. Its displacement will be _____.

6. Its velocity will be _____.

7. Which direction will the automobile move if it travels on the route labeled B? _____

8. Its displacement will be _____.

9. Its velocity will be _____.

10. Which direction will the automobile move if it travels on the route labeled C? _____

11. Its displacement will be _____.

12. Its velocity will be _____.

13. Draw an arrow labeled D to show the displacement of the automobile if it moved west.

14. Draw an arrow labeled E to show the displacement of the automobile if it moved southwest.

15. Draw an arrow labeled F to show the displacement of the automobile if it moved northeast.

Name _____ Date _____

IDENTIFYING SPEED OR VELOCITY

Speed refers to rate of motion. Velocity refers to rate of motion and direction. Each of the statements below describes speed or velocity. Place an "s" in the blank if the statement refers to speed or a "v" if it refers to velocity.

_____ 1. Emily was driving northeast at a speed of 60 mph.

_____ 2. The train was traveling at a speed of 70 mph.

_____ 3. The average speed of a passenger plane is 400 mph.

_____ 4. Sally drove at a speed of 50 mph south for two hours, and then she turned east and her speed was 60 mph.

_____ 5. Two planes leave the same airport. One plane is flying east at a speed of 300 mph. The other plane is flying south at a speed of 350 mph.

_____ 6. The sprinter ran the 100 meters in 10 seconds.

_____ 7. Emily rode her horse 2 hours and traveled 4 miles.

SPEED AND VELOCITY IN MILES AND KILOMETERS

Speed and velocity are often expressed in kilometers per hour rather than miles per hour. There are 1.6 kilometers in a mile. So if one travels ten miles, he or she travels 16 kilometers (10 miles * 1.6 = 16 kilometers). There are 0.62 miles in a kilometer. So if one travels 10 kilometers, he or she travels 6.2 miles (10 kilometers * 0.62 = 6.2 miles).

Fill in the blanks in the table below by figuring the miles per hour or kilometers per hour and converting from miles to kilometers or kilometers to miles.

	Miles	Time	Speed		Kilometers	Time	Speed
1.	100	2 hrs.	50 mph	=	160	2 hrs.	80 kph
2.	10	1 hr.	_____	=	16	1 hr.	_____
3.	1,000	20 hrs.	_____	=	_____	20 hrs.	_____
4.	2,000	_____	40 mph	=	3,200	_____	64 kph
5.	500	10 hrs.	_____	=	_____	_____	_____
6.	_____	2 hrs.	_____	=	8	2 hrs.	4 kph

Name _____ Date _____

DETERMINING SPEED, TIME, AND DISTANCE

Speed, time, and distance are important in solving problems. If two of the three are known, the other can be found.

Examples:

1. To find speed, divide:
   Speed = Distance/Time   Speed = 200 miles/5 hrs.   40 mph = 200/5
2. To find distance, multiply:
   Distance = Speed*Time   Miles = 40 mph*5 hrs.   200 miles = 40*5
3. To find time, divide:
   Time = Distance/Speed   Time = 200 miles/40 mph   5 hours = 200/40

Solve the following. Fill in the blank or circle the correct answer.

1. Emily and her friends are traveling from Arizona to California. The distance is 400 miles. They intend to average 50 mph. Looking at speed, distance, and time, you know the (a) _____ and (b) _____. You do not know the (c) _____.

2. Which example from above will you use to solve Problem #1?   (a) 1   (b) 2   (c) 3

3. The answer to #1 is _____ .

4. Emily, Stephany, and Megan are traveling from California to Illinois. They intend to average 50 mph. They are told it will take them 40 hours at that speed. Looking at speed, distance, and time, you know the (a) _____ and (b) _____. You do not know the (c)_____.

5. Which example from above will you use to solve Problem #4?   (a) 1   (b) 2   (c) 3

6. The answer to #4 is _____ .

7. Emily and her friends are traveling from Illinois to Arizona. The distance is 1,800 miles. They intend to drive the distance in 30 hours. Looking at speed, distance, and time, you know the (a) _____ and (b) _____ . You do not know the (c) _____ .

8. Which example from above will you use to solve Problem #7?   (a) 1   (b) 2   (c) 3

9. The answer to #7 is _____ .

Name _____ Date _____

USING GRAPHS TO ILLUSTRATE DISTANCE AND TIME

In science, data is often plotted on a graph. Data relating to speed and velocity are often plotted on special graphs that show specific relationships.

One such graph for plotting information related to speed is a **distance/time** graph. The distance/time graph below shows the distance one might travel by train, plane, and bicycle for different times.

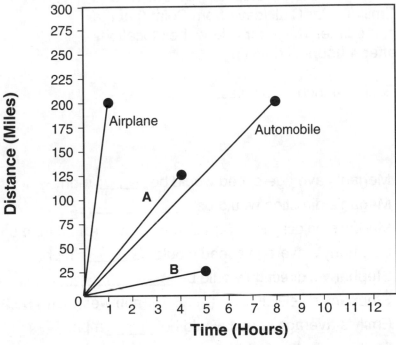

Refer to the distance/time graph and answer the following questions. Circle the correct answer and/or fill in the blank.

1. The airplane has traveled   (a) 100   (b) 150   (c) 200 miles   in (d) _____ hours.

2. The automobile has traveled   (a) 75   (b) 100   (c) 200 miles   in (d) _____ hours.

3. The line representing the distance traveled by a bicycle would likely be   (a) line A   (b) line B.

4. The airplane is averaging _____ miles per hour.

5. The automobile is averaging _____ miles per hour.

6. Extend the line for the airplane to show where the line will end after the plane has flown 1½ hours.

7. After completing #6, the airplane will have traveled a total of _____ miles.

8. Extend the line for the automobile to show where the line ends after the car has traveled another 3 hours.

9. After completing #8, the automobile will have traveled a total of _____ miles.

Name _____ Date _____

USING DIAGRAMS TO ILLUSTRATE SPEED AND VELOCITY

Diagrams may be used to show data about speed and velocity.

Refer to the diagram below and answer the following questions.

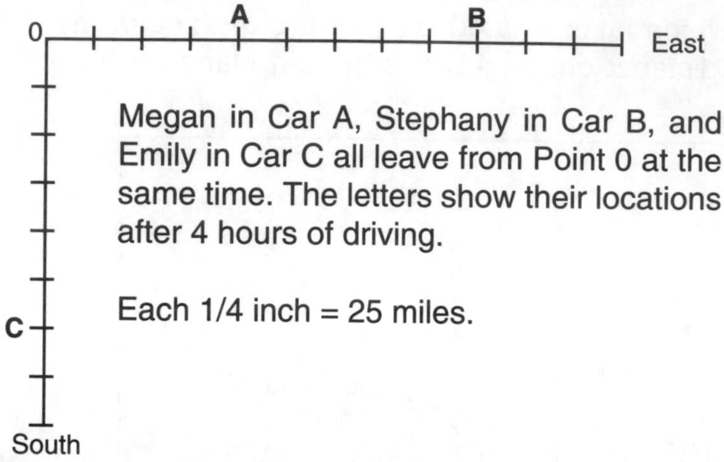

Megan in Car A, Stephany in Car B, and Emily in Car C all leave from Point 0 at the same time. The letters show their locations after 4 hours of driving.

Each 1/4 inch = 25 miles.

1. After 4 hours of driving, Megan's average speed would be _____ mph.
2. After 4 hours of driving, Megan's direction would be _____.
3. After 4 hours of driving, Megan's velocity is   (a) 25 mph east   (b) 25 mph south.
4. After 4 hours of driving, Stephany's average speed would be _____ mph.
5. After 4 hours of driving, Stephany's direction would be _____.
6. After 4 hours of driving, Stephany's velocity is   (a) 56.25 mph west   (b) 56.25 mph east.
7. After 4 hours of driving, Emily's average speed would be _____ mph.
8. After 4 hours of driving, Emily's direction would be _____.
9. After 4 hours of driving, Emily's velocity is   (a) 37.5 mph north   (b) 37.5 mph south.

MOTION MATCHING

Match the definition in Column B with the correct term in Column A.

COLUMN A	COLUMN B
_____ 1. Acceleration	A. Distance traveled by a moving object in a given time
_____ 2. Centripetal Acceleration	B. Rate of change in speed with time
_____ 3. Deceleration	C. Refers to a body moving
_____ 4. Displacement	D. Speed in a specific direction
_____ 5. Motion	E. When a body in motion loses speed
_____ 6. Speed	F. Acceleration associated with circular motion
_____ 7. Velocity	G. The distance and direction an object is from a fixed point

Name _____ Date _____

Understanding Scalar and Vector Quantities

Scalar quantities have magnitude only. These are quantities that may be expressed by a single number. Scalar quantities include quantities of **mass, length, weight, density, volume,** and **time.** Each **scalar** quantity must be expressed in the appropriate units, like **amount, distance, size,** or **rate.** These units are called scalars.

For example:
1. The dimensions of a room are 12 feet by 10 feet. The number of square feet in the room is 120.
2. A car that travels 300 miles in 5 hours is traveling at a speed of 60 miles per hour.

Vector quantities are quantities which have both magnitude and direction. Vector quantities are expressed in appropriate units along with a vector or arrow that shows direction. The vectors (arrows) are divided into units of length that indicate the **magnitude** of the vector quantity. The **direction** of the arrow indicates the direction of the vector.

For example, in the diagram below, the arrow shows magnitude and direction. The length of the line shows magnitude, and the arrow shows the direction quantity. The magnitude is indicated by $\frac{1}{4}''$ marks, each equal to 25 miles or a total magnitude of 250 miles. The arrow shows the direction is east. The magnitude is 250 miles and the direction is east.

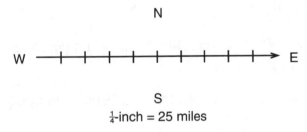

$\frac{1}{4}$-inch = 25 miles

1. Draw a vector in the space below with a magnitude of 400 miles and a direction that is west. Choose your own scale.

Refer to the vectors at right and complete the questions that follow.

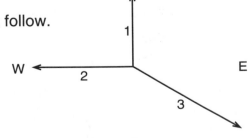

Each $\frac{1}{4}$-inch equals 40 miles.

2. The vector marked "1" has a magnitude of (a) _____ miles and a direction of (b) _____ .

3. The vector marked "2" has a magnitude of (a) _____ miles and a direction of (b) _____ .

4. The vector marked "3" has a magnitude of (a) _____ miles and a direction of (b) _____ .

Name _____ Date _____

USING VECTORS TO PLOT DISPLACEMENT

An important term in describing the direction of motion is **displacement**. The displacement of an object is the object's distance and direction from a given location. The distance is often stated in miles, kilometers, or meters and the direction as north, south, east, or west.

To plot displacement, a diagram is used showing a north-south and an east-west line. The magnitude of the displacement is shown using vectors. For magnitude to be shown accurately, the diagram must represent a specific scale.

Complete the following activity. Draw your vectors below.

Draw a $2\frac{1}{2}$-inch line from points A to B. Mark each $\frac{1}{4}$-inch on the line with a dot (•). Place an upward-pointing arrow on the line at the dot that marks 2 inches.

Draw a $2\frac{1}{2}$-inch line from points A to C. Mark each $\frac{1}{4}$-inch on the line with a dot (•). Place a right-pointing arrow on the line at the dot that marks $1\frac{3}{4}$ inches.

Draw a vertical line $2\frac{1}{2}$ inches from the tip of the arrow on line A-C. Place the letter D at the end of the line. Mark each $\frac{1}{4}$-inch with a dot. Place an upward-pointing arrow on the dot marking 2 inches.

Draw a horizontal dashed line from the tip of the arrow on line A-B to D on the vertical line. You should have formed a rectangle.

Draw a line from A to D. Mark the line at each $\frac{1}{4}$-inch with a dot (•). Place an outward-pointing arrow on the line at D.

Center one-fourth inch below line A-C the statement, "Each $\frac{1}{4}$-inch equals 25 miles."

<u>N</u>

B
•

•

<u>W</u>   <u>E</u>

•
A   •
                                                 C

<u>S</u>

Name _____   Date _____

USING VECTORS TO PLOT DISPLACEMENT (CONTINUED)

Refer to the completed rectangle on the previous page and answer the following questions. Fill in the blanks or circle the correct answer.

1. The distance represented by vector A-B is _____ miles.

2. The arrow on vector A-B points toward the   (a) north   (b) south   (c) east   (d) west.

3. The magnitude of vector A-B is   (a) 50   (b) 100   (c) 175   (d) 200 miles.

4. The direction of vector A-B is   (a) north   (b) south   (c) east   (d) west.

5. The vector A-B is correctly labeled   (a) N, 150 miles   (b) S, 150 miles   (c) N, 200 miles (d) S, 200 miles.

6. The distance represented by vector A-C is _____ miles.

7. The arrow on vector A-C points toward the   (a) north   (b) south   (c) east   (d) west.

8. The magnitude of vector A-C is   (a) 50   (b) 100   (c) 175   (d) 300 miles.

9. The direction of the vector A-C is   (a) north   (b) south   (c) east   (d) west.

10. The vector A-C is correctly labeled   (a) E, 150 miles   (b) E, 175 miles   (c) W, 250 miles (d) W, 175 miles.

11. The distance represented by vector A-D is _____ miles.

12. The arrow on vector A-D points toward the   (a) northeast   (b) southeast   (c) northwest (d) southwest.

13. The magnitude of vector A-D is (a) 50   (b) 100   (c) 175   (d) 275 miles.

14. The direction of the vector A-D is   (a) northeast   (b) southeast   (c) northwest   (d) southwest.

15. The vector A-D is correctly labeled   (a) NE, 275 miles   (b) NE, 175 miles   (c) NE, 250 miles (d) NE, 175 miles.

Name _____ Date _____

Understanding Simple Machines

Machines help man do work. To understand simple machines, it is important to understand how **work** and **power** are defined in science. In the activities that follow, you will find the terms "work" and "power" have very specific meanings.

THE SCIENTIFIC MEANING OF WORK

Refer to the definition for work below and complete the following exercise. First, place a check on the blanks below each statement to determine if the statement fulfills the requirements for the definition of work. Then, place a (+) on the blank if work is done. Place a (-) on the blank if no work is performed.

Definition for work: **A force is applied to an object, and the object moves as a result of the force.**

_____ 1. You push a desk across the room.
   ___ A force was applied.
   ___ The object moves as a result of a force.

_____ 2. You ride your bicycle to school.
   ___ A force was applied.
   ___ The object moves as a result of the force.

_____ 3. You try to move a large boulder by pushing it. After ten minutes of hard pushing, you find the boulder has not moved.
   ___ A force was applied.
   ___ The object moves as a result of the force.

_____ 4. You stand for 15 minutes, holding a box of books for a friend.
   ___ A force was applied.
   ___ The object moves as a result of the force.

_____ 5. You and a friend are hired to move a cord of wood. Both of you have other jobs. You will be able to work before lunch, and your friend will finish the job after lunch. When you leave at lunch, you have moved half of the cord of wood to the new location. When your friend arrives after lunch, he mistakenly moves the wood you have moved back to the original location of the cord of wood.
   ___ A force was applied by you and your friend to move the wood.
   ___ The object moves as a result of the force applied by you and your friend.

6. When the individual who had hired you and your friend to move the cord of wood found the wood back in its original location, he refused to pay you for your time. It was his opinion that no work had been accomplished. On the blanks below, explain why you did or did not perform work.

_____

_____

_____

Name _____   Date _____

MEASURING WORK IN THE ENGLISH AND METRIC SYSTEMS

When simple machines, such as the lever, pulley, screw, and wedge, are used, it is important to **measure the work** that is done. There is a specific formula that is used to measure work. The formula is **work = force*distance.** This formula says the amount of work done is determined by multiplying the force applied by the distance the object moves.

When measuring the amount of work performed, it is important to determine how the work will be measured. Work may be measured using the **English system** or the **metric system**.

Measuring work using the English system: In the English system, measurement is in foot-pounds. The formula work = force*distance becomes **work = feet*pounds**.

Measuring work using the metric system: In the metric system, measurement is in newton-meters. This is also called a **Joule**. The formula work = force*distance becomes **work = newtons*meters**.

When using the metric system to measure the amount of work performed, work is usually measured as meter/kilogram/second. To determine the amount of work performed, it is necessary to multiply newtons times meters, so in the metric system, the formula becomes **work = newtons*meters**.

Answer the following. Circle the correct choice.

1. In the metric formula, newtons refers to the (distance/force).
2. In the metric formula, meters refers to the (distance/force).

To understand the metric measurements, you will compare the English system to the metric system in the activities that follow.

metric system
1 meter equals 39.37 inches
100 centimeters equals 1 meter

English system
1 inch equals 2.54 centimeters
1 yard equals 36 inches

Complete the following. Circle the correct choice.

3. A meter is approximately   (a) 5   (b) 2   (c) 3   (d) 8   inches longer than a yard.
4. One foot equals approximately   (a) 30.5   (b) 60   (c) 40   (d) 10 centimeters.
5. One inch is   (a) $\frac{1}{3}$ (b) $\frac{1}{12}$ (c) $\frac{1}{36}$ (d) $\frac{1}{10}$ of a yard.
6. One centimeter is   (a) $\frac{1}{10}$ (b) $\frac{1}{100}$ (c) $\frac{1}{4}$ (d) $\frac{1}{3}$ of a meter.
7. One-half of a meter equals _____ centimeters.
8. One yard equals _____ centimeters.

41

Name _____ Date _____

REVIEWING THE MEASUREMENT OF WORK

Use the terms below to fill in the blanks in the following selection.

work   **metric**   **English**   **distance**   **force**
newton-meters   **simple machines**   **foot-pounds**

In science, the only time (1) _____ is performed is when an object is moved a specific distance. In the English system, the amount of work performed is measured in (2) _____ - _____. In the metric system, the amount of work performed is measured in (3) _____ - _____ .

Work in science is measured using the (4) _____ or (5) _____ system. The formula for work is **work = (6)** _____ * **(7)** _____ . The lever, pulley, screw, and wedge are all examples of (8) _____ _____ that help people perform work.

Match the definitions in Column B with the terms in Column A.

Column A	**Column B**
_____ 9. English measurement	A. 2.54 centimeters
_____ 10. Metric measurement	B. When a force moves an object a specific distance
_____ 11. Joule	C. 39.37 inches
_____ 12. Equals one inch	D. Foot-pound measurement
_____ 13. Equals one meter	E. Meter/kilogram/second measurement
_____ 14. Work	F. Newton*meter

Solve the following.

15. A man lifts a box weighing 50 pounds 2 feet off the floor. The force is   (a) _____ . The distance is   (b) _____ . The work performed is **w = fd**, so   (c) **w =** _____ * ____ and (d) **w =** _____ foot-pounds.

16. A gymnast weighs 140 pounds. Using only his hands and arms, the gymnast climbs 5 feet up a rope. The force is   (a) _____ . The distance is   (b) _____ . The work performed is **w = fd**. (c) **w =** ____ * ____ and   (d) **w =** _____ .

17. A boy weighing 120 pounds climbs stairs that are 10 feet high. The force is   (a) _____ . The distance is   (b) _____ . The work performed is   (c) ___ = _____ * _____ . The work performed by the boy is   (d) _____ .

Name _____ Date _____

THE SCIENTIFIC MEANING OF POWER

The definition for **work** is an important term to understand in physical science. Another important term is **power**. **Power refers to how long it takes to complete a given amount of work.** Write the term "work" or "power" on the blank before each of the definitions below.

1. _____ Refers to how long it takes to do a particular job
2. _____ Refers to the force needed to move an object a specific distance
3. _____ Stephany lifts a sack of beans three feet off the floor and places it on the shelf.
4. _____ Megan lifts a sack of beans three feet off the floor and places it on a shelf in four seconds.

The formula for determining the **power** or **rate** of doing work is **power = work divided by time, or P = W/t.** Work, or "W" in the formula, refers to the energy used. Time, or "t", is the time that passes while the energy is being used.

Power is stated as horsepower. Engines in automobiles are rated as so many horsepower. The measurement of horsepower was developed by James Watt at a time when horses were used rather than machines. Watt measured the rate at which a horse could perform work. He found the rate to be 550 foot-pounds per second or 550 ft. lbs./sec.

5. Emily thought about a weight lifter she had seen on television. The weight lifter lifted 550 pounds from the floor and held it over his head. The distance the 550 pounds was lifted was 8 feet. The weight lifter held the weight above his head for three seconds before dropping the weight. Emily thought the following was true. Do you agree? Write "agree" or "disagree" on the blanks before each statement and then explain your answer.

_____ (a) The weight lifter did work because he applied a force to lift the weights when he moved the weights a specific distance. I (agree/disagree) because _____

_____

_____ (b) The weight lifter did not do any work while holding the weight over his head for three seconds. I (agree/disagree) because _____

_____

6. Megan said she did not think the weight lifter performed any work. Do you agree or disagree with Megan's thinking in the statement below?

_____ (a) When the weights were dropped back to the floor, the weights were back in the original position. The weight lifter performed no work because the weights had not been moved a specific distance. I (agree/disagree) because _____

_____

_____ (b) If the weight lifter would have placed the weights on a rack that was four feet high, work would have been performed. I (agree/disagree) because _____

_____

43

Name _____ Date _____

THE SCIENTIFIC MEANING OF POWER (CONTINUED)

_____ (c) In determining the amount of work performed, the distance the weights were moved was four feet, not eight feet. I (agree/disagree) because _____

_____

7. Emily and Megan wanted to find out how much power the weight lifter used in lifting the weights. Place a plus (+) in front of the statements below that contain things Emily and Megan would need to know to determine the amount of power the weight lifter used.

_____ (a) The distance the weights were moved

_____ (b) The height of the weight lifter

_____ (c) The force used to move the weights

_____ (d) The time it took to move the weights the given distance

_____ (e) The weight of the weight lifter

8. Stephany said that to determine the power the weight lifter used, the formula **power = work/time**, or **P = W/t**, could be used. Before each of Stephany's statements, write agree or disagree. Write why you agree or disagree on the following blanks.

_____ a) It would be necessary to determine the amount of work the weight lifter did. I (agree/disagree) because _____

_____

_____ b) Work is determined by multiplying force by distance. I (agree/disagree) because

_____

_____

_____ c) Another way of writing the formula P = W/t would be P = f*d/t. I (agree/disagree) because _____

_____

9. Emily found that it had taken the weight lifter five seconds to lift the 550 pounds four feet. To determine the power used, she thought it would be necessary to complete each of the following steps. Complete the steps for Emily.

   (a) The formula for work is **W = f*d**. To find the work performed, multiply 550 pounds by four feet. 550*4 = _____ foot-pounds

   (b) The formula for power is **P = W/t** or **P = f*d/t**. The amount of work performed must be placed in the formula. **P = _____/t**.

   (c) The amount of work and time must be placed in the formula. **P = _____ / _____**.

   (d) The power used by the weight lifter to lift the 550 pounds four feet in five seconds is _____ foot-pounds per second.

Name _____ Date _____

WORK AND POWER: WHAT DO YOU THINK?

1. Emily, Stephany, and Megan were told to carry boxes of books from the first floor to the second floor in their school. Each of them were to carry two boxes. Each box weighed 20 pounds. The second floor was 10 feet above the first floor. Each of them did   (a) 400   (b) 10   (c) 100   (d) 0 foot-pounds of work. (Circle the correct answer.)

2. It took Emily 5 minutes, Stephany 6 minutes, and Megan 8 minutes to carry the two boxes of books from the first to the second floor. Indicate whether each of the following statements is true or false. On the blank below each statement, tell why the statement is true or false.

_____ (a) Emily did more work than Stephany.

_____

_____ (b) Emily did more work than Megan.

_____

_____ (c) Emily, Megan, and Stephany did the same amount of work.

_____

3. It took Emily 5 minutes, Stephany 6 minutes, and Megan 8 minutes to carry the two boxes of books from the first to the second floor. Indicate whether each of the following statements is true or false. On the blank below each statement, tell why the statement is true or false.

_____ (a) Emily exerted more power than Stephany.

_____

_____ (b) Emily exerted more power than Megan.

_____

_____ (c) Emily, Megan, and Stephany exerted the same amount of power.

_____

4. Each of the statements below refers to work or power. Write "work" or "power" on the blank before each statement.

_____ (a) Refers to how long it takes to do a particular job
_____ (b) Refers to the force needed to move an object a specific distance

Name _____ Date _____

SIMPLE MACHINES

Man invented simple machines to perform work that is not possible by muscles alone. Machines help man move objects in a specific direction as a result of a force that is applied. Simple machines provide more power than man. Simple machines include the **lever, wedge, screw, pulleys, inclined plane,** and **the wheel and axle.** These machines help man apply a force and make work easier. In some cases, the machines are used to increase the speed and distance of a force.

The terms **mechanical advantage, efficiency, effort,** and **resistance** are important terms in understanding simple machines. **Mechanical advantage** refers to the number of times the force applied is multiplied. The **force** applied to the machine is called the **effort.** The **force** must overcome the **resistance** of the object that is to be moved. Mechanical advantage is determined by the relationship between effort and resistance (load).

Stephany, in Diagram B, must move the box without the help of a simple machine. Megan, in Diagram A, uses a lever. The force applied to move the box is the effort indicated by the direction of the arrow. The resistance (load) to the effort force is the resistance (load) of the box to be moved.

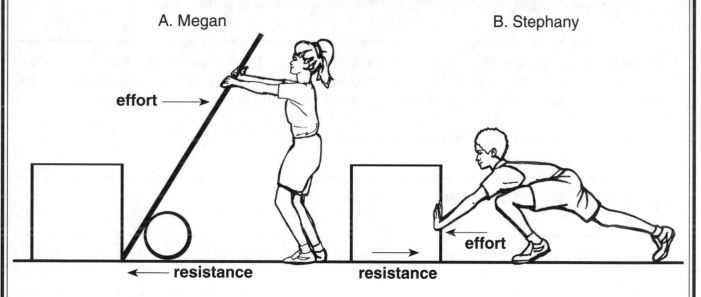

A. Megan   B. Stephany

effort →

← resistance   resistance

What do you think? (Both boxes offer the same resistance.) Circle the correct choice and complete the statement.

1. (Megan/Stephany) will use less effort to move the box because _____

_____ .

Name _____ Date _____

SIMPLE MACHINES (CONTINUED)

Emily decided to help Stephany. She told Stephany the lever gave Megan a mechanical advantage. Emily suggested Stephany use a lever. Emily helped Stephany place the lever under the box.

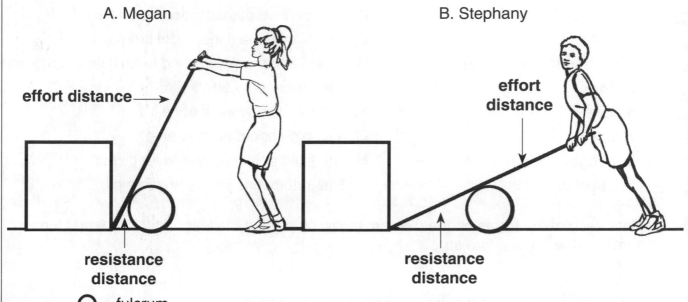

A. Megan   B. Stephany

effort distance →

effort distance

resistance distance   **resistance distance**

◯ = fulcrum

effort distance = length of lever from fulcrum to Megan/Stephany
resistance distance = length of lever from fulcrum to box

Circle the correct choice:

2. The lever (will/will not) help Stephany move the box.

3. The lever Stephany uses (will/will not) move the box easier than the lever used by Megan.

4. (Megan/Stephany) will have to use the greater effort to move the box.

5. (Megan's/Stephany's) lever will move the box the greatest distance.

Mechanical advantage is found by dividing the distance the resistance (load) moves by the distance the effort force moves. The formula is **Mechanical Advantage = distance resistance moves (load)/distance effort force moves (effort)** or **MA = rd/ed**.

Determine the mechanical advantage of the levers used by Megan and Stephany.

Stephany's lever: effort distance = 5 feet   resistance distance = 4 feet
Megan's lever: effort distance = 8 feet   resistance distance = 2 feet

6. The mechanical advantage of Stephany's lever is MA = _____ / _____.   MA = _____.

7. The mechanical advantage of Megan's lever is MA = _____ / _____.   MA = _____.

Name _____ Date _____

REVIEWING WORK, POWER, AND SIMPLE MACHINES

Match the definitions in Column B with the correct terms in Column A.

COLUMN A	COLUMN B
_____ 1. fulcrum	A. A rope around a wheel is an example.
_____ 2. inclined plane	B. Two inclined planes placed together
_____ 3. lever	C. This simple machine is like a pole.
_____ 4. mechanical advantage	D. Wheel and crank attached to an axle
_____ 5. power	E. Load divided by effort
_____ 6. pulley	F. The rate that work is done
_____ 7. screw	G. A sloping board is an example.
_____ 8. wedge	H. The fixed point where a lever pivots
_____ 9. wheel and axle	I. The automobile jack is an example.

10. Locate each of the terms on the diagram below by placing the letter or color for that term on the diagram in the appropriate spot.

    (a) resistance arm
    (b) resistance distance: color the resistance distance red
    (c) resistance force (load)
    (d) effort arm
    (e) effort force
    (f) effort distance: color the effort distance blue
    (g) fulcrum

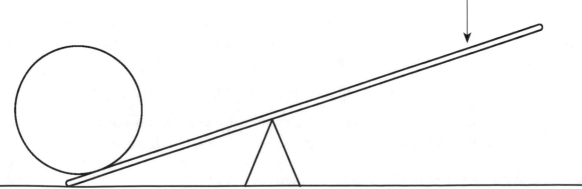

Name _____ Date _____

Understanding Solids, Liquids, and Gases

Solids, liquids, and gases have definite characteristics. A **solid** has a definite **shape** and **volume**. Solids resist being pulled apart. Another characteristic is **elasticity**. Elasticity means that a solid can be bent or twisted a limited amount, and it will return to its former shape. Solids are also **malleable**, which means the solid can be formed into a new shape. Gold is a solid that can easily be hammered into a thin sheet that is still a solid.

A liquid has a **definite volume** but takes the **shape** of the container holding it. When water is poured from one container into a container shaped differently, the water takes the shape of the new container. However, the surface of the water remains **horizontal** no matter what the shape of the container. Liquids have **surface tension**, and this surface tension causes the liquid to form drops. Liquids also have **capillarity**. When a thin straw or glass tube is dipped in a liquid, the liquid will rise slightly in the straw or glass tube.

A gas has neither a definite **shape** nor **volume**. A gas will **expand** and fill any container in which it is placed.

Complete the following activity. Each statement refers to a solid, liquid, or gas. Place the letter S (solid), L (liquid), or G (gas) on the blank before each statement.

_____ 1. Will expand and fill the container into which it is placed

_____ 2. Has a definite shape

_____ 3. Is malleable, which means the shape can be changed into a new shape

_____ 4. Surface tension is evident when drops are formed.

_____ 5. Has neither a definite shape nor definite volume

_____ 6. The shape changes when placed in a new container, but the surface remains horizontal.

_____ 7. A small straw can be used to demonstrate capillarity.

_____ 8. When slightly bent or twisted, it will return to the original shape.

9. The following are a solid, a liquid, and a gas. List the characteristics for each.

Nail: _____

_____

_____

Water: _____

_____

_____

Oxygen: _____

_____

_____

Name _____ Date _____

Understanding Temperature and Heat

A material may be in the solid state at one temperature, the liquid state at a higher temperature, and the gaseous state at an even higher temperature. Water occurs in the liquid state, ice occurs in the solid state, and water vapor occurs in the gaseous state. In science, the use of temperature to measure the various states of matter is important. Thermometers are measurement tools used in understanding solids, liquids, and gases.

In science, heat and temperature are not the same thing. They are related in that increasing or decreasing the heat changes the temperature. **Temperature is a measurement. Heat refers to the transfer of energy from one object to another.**

When heat is added to an object, the temperature rises. When enough heat is added to water, the temperature rises, and when the temperature reaches a certain point, some of the water will change from the liquid state to the gaseous state.

Heat is measured in calories. **A calorie is the amount of heat that will raise one gram of water one Celsius degree in temperature.** Another term associated with heat is the British Thermal Unit or BTU. **A BTU is the amount of heat needed to raise the temperature of one pound of water one degree Fahrenheit.**

Fill in the blanks in the exercise below.

Heat refers to the transfer of (1)_____. If heat is added to an object, the (2) _____ rises. When the temperature of an object becomes high enough, it may change from a (3) _____ to a (4) _____ or to a (5) _____.

THERMOMETERS

Temperature can be measured with a thermometer. Thermometers are made in different ways. Many thermometers are made with a sealed glass tube that has a liquid, such as mercury or colored alcohol, inside. The glass tube is then calibrated so the temperature can be read. Other thermometers have two different types of metal fastened together. The two metals often used are a strip of iron and a strip of brass. The pieces of iron and brass are fastened together and a bimetallic strip is formed. The two different metals expand and contract differently when the temperature changes. The bimetallic strip is attached to a pointer that moves and lets you read the temperature. This type of thermometer is used commonly to adjust furnaces in homes.

Match the definitions in Column B with the terms in Column A.

COLUMN A	COLUMN B
_____ 1. Thermometer	A. Liquid used in glass-sealed thermometer to show the temperature
_____ 2. Bimetallic strip	B. Instrument used to measure the temperature
_____ 3. Expand	C. Two different kinds of metal fastened together
_____ 4. Contract	D. Means the volume of the material has increased
_____ 5. Mercury	E. Means the volume of the material has decreased

Name _____ Date _____

MEASURING TEMPERATURE WITH FAHRENHEIT, CELSIUS, AND KELVIN SCALES

In science, the use of temperature is very important. To understand temperature, it is important to know about temperature scales. Temperature scales may be **Fahrenheit, Celsius,** or **Kelvin** scales.

- The Fahrenheit scale is calibrated so the temperatures can be read from 0° to +212° and from 0° to -459°. Two important temperatures on the Fahrenheit scale are +32° and +212°. The temperature at which water will freeze is +32°. The temperature at which water will boil is +212°.

- The Celcius scale is calibrated so the temperatures can be read from 0° to +100° and from 0° to -273°. Two important temperatures on the Celsius scale are 0° and 100°. The temperature at which water will freeze is 0°. The temperature at which water will boil is 100°.

- The Kelvin scale is calibrated so temperatures can be read from 0 K to +273 K. Notice the numbers on the Kelvin scale are followed by the letter "K", not " ° ", the symbol for degrees. Zero is the coldest temperature that can be recorded on the Kelvin scale.

Complete the blanks in the following selection with the correct words from the paragraphs above.

The three temperature scales are the (1) _____ , (2) _____, and (3) _____ scales. The Fahrenheit scale and (4) _____ scale measure temperature in degrees. The Kelvin scale uses the letter (5) "___" following each number on the scale. The (6) _____ scale is calibrated so that water freezes at a temperature of 32° and boils at a temperature of (7) _____ °. The (8) _____ scale is calibrated so that water freezes at 0° and boils at (9) _____ °.

Read the following and circle the correct answers to the questions below.

Two important temperatures on the Fahrenheit scale are +32° and +212°. The temperature at which water will freeze is +32°. The temperature at which water will boil is +212°. Two important temperatures on the Celsius scale are 0° and 100°. The temperature at which water will freeze is 0°. The temperature at which water will boil is 100°.

10. The number of degrees between the freezing and boiling points on the Celsius scale is
(a) 50°   (b) 100°   (c) 80°   (d) 10°.

11. The number of degrees between the freezing and boiling points on the Fahrenheit scale is
(a) 100°   (b) 50°   (c) 180°   (d) 80°.

12. Place the answer in #11 over the answer in #10 to make a fraction. The fraction is
(a) $\frac{100}{220}$ (b) $\frac{100}{32}$ (c) $\frac{100}{180}$ (d) $\frac{180}{100}$.

13. The answer in #12 equals the **simple fraction**   (a) $\frac{5}{11}$ (b) $\frac{25}{8}$ (c) $\frac{5}{9}$ (d) $\frac{9}{5}$.

14. One degree in Celsius equals   (a) 2.0   (b) 1.8   (c) 4.0   (d) 5.0   on the Fahrenheit scale.

Name _____ Date _____

TEMPERATURE SCALE CONVERSIONS

Below are examples of thermometers that illustrate how temperatures are calibrated on Fahrenheit and Celsius (Centigrade) scales.

Celsius:

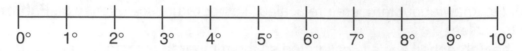

Fahrenheit:

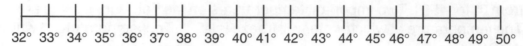

Refer to the scales above and answer the following questions.

1. Zero degrees on the Celsius scale is read as ____ ° on the Fahrenheit scale.

2. Ten degrees on the Celsius scale is read as ____ ° on the Fahrenheit scale.

3. The number of degrees between 32° and 50° is ____ ° on the Fahrenheit scale.

4. The number of degrees between 0° and 10° on the Celsius scale is ____ °.

5. Divide the answer in #3 by the answer in #4. The answer is ____ °.

6. You have found that: (circle the correct answer)

    (a) each degree on the Celsius scale equals 2 degrees on the Fahrenheit scale.

    (b) each degree on the Celsius scale equals 3 degrees on the Fahrenheit scale.

    (c) each degree on the Celsius scale equals 2.5 degrees on the Fahrenheit scale.

    (d) each degree on the Celsius scale equals 1.8 degrees on the Fahrenheit scale.

It is often necessary to convert a Fahrenheit temperature reading to a Celsius temperature reading or Celsius to Fahrenheit. There are formulas for making these conversions.

To convert Fahrenheit to Celsius, use the formula: C = (F - 32)*5/9.
Example: Convert 50°F to Celsius.   C = (50° - 32)*5/9 = 18*5/9 = 10°C.

Convert the following Fahrenheit temperatures to Celsius. Show all steps.

7. 77°F   C = (____ - 32°)*5/9 =____ *5/9 =____ ° C

8. 212°F   C = (____ - ____)*5/___ = ____ * ___ / ___ = ___ ° C

To convert Celsius to Fahrenheit, use the formula: F = (C*9/5) + 32.
Example: Convert 10°C to Fahrenheit.   F = (10°*9/5) + 32 = 18 + 32 = 50°F.

Convert the following Celsius temperatures to Fahrenheit. Show all steps.

9. 25°C   F = (____ *9/5) + 32 =____ + 32 =____ °F

10. 0°C   F = (____ * ___ / ___) + ____ = ____ + ____ = ____ ° F

Name _____ Date _____

Understanding Wave Action

When a pebble is dropped into the water, the wave motion is easily seen. However, not all waves can be seen. Sound waves that move through the air cannot be seen. Electric waves, also, cannot be seen.

Waves move through water and air. Water and air are known as **mediums** through which waves move. The density and temperature of the medium the wave is moving through determines the speed of the wave.

Complete the following activity. On the diagram below, color the part above the boundary line red and the part below the boundary line blue. Answer the questions that follow.

Air

_____ Boundary Line

Water

1. The medium above the boundary line is _____.

2. The medium below the boundary line is _____ .

Fill in the following blanks by using the words below.

Light	type	distance	medium	travel
air	speeds	Sound	water	

Waves travel at different (3) _____, depending on the (4) _____ the wave is passing through. Each type of wave travels a given (5) _____ in a given period of time. It is the (6) _____ of wave that determines the speed. Waves (7) _____ at a specific speed. (8) _____ waves travel 1,100 feet per second. (9) _____ waves travel 186,000 miles per second.

In the above diagram, the mediums are (10) _____ and (11) _____ .

Name _____ Date _____

LONGITUDINAL AND TRANSVERSE WAVES

When waves move through a medium, the waves formed may be **longitudinal** waves or **transverse** waves.

Longitudinal waves:

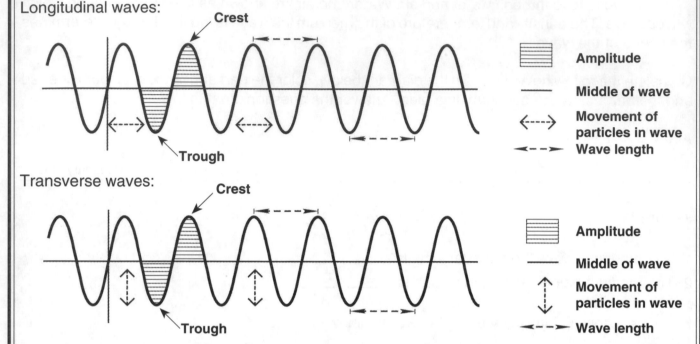

Transverse waves:

The diagram of longitudinal and transverse waves will help you complete the matching exercise below. Match each definition in Column B with the correct term in Column A.

COLUMN A

_____ 1. Amplitude

_____ 2. Frequency

_____ 3. Longitudinal

_____ 4. Transverse

_____ 5. Wavelength

_____ 6. Period

_____ 7. Crest

_____ 8. Trough

_____ 9. Particles

_____ 10. Medium

COLUMN B

A. Refers to number of waves passing a given point in a period of time

B. Maximum displacement of vibrating particles in the medium

C. Refers to air, water, etc. that waves move through

D. Refers to the high point of a wave

E. Refers to maximum downward motion by a particle in a wave

F. Wave where motion of particles in medium is up and down

G. Wave where motion of particles in medium is horizontal

H. Distance between two consecutive corresponding points in the wave

I. Distance from center of wave to point of greatest displacement

J. The movement of these differ in longitudinal and transverse waves.

Name _____ Date _____

WAVE SPEED

It is important to note that all waves move at specific speeds. Waves move at different speeds depending on the mediums through which they are moving. For example, a wave moving through water moves at a different speed than a wave moving through air. The speed of a wave depends on the length of the wave and the frequency (number) of waves passing a given point in one second.

On the diagram below, the wavelength from "a" to "b" is two meters. In the diagram, each wave is labeled "a", "b", and so on and numbered w1, w2, and so on.

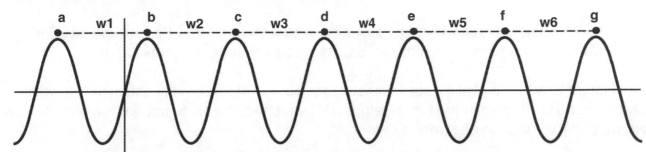

Assume you are standing on a dock and watching the waves pass directly below where you are standing. You count the number of seconds it takes for w1, w2, w3, and w4 to pass directly below you. You determine that all four waves pass below you in two seconds.

Answer the following questions.

For questions 1 and 2, choose your answers from the following four terms.

| **maximum** | **crest** | **minimum** | **trough** |

1. The distance from "a" to "b" includes a _____ and _____ .

2. The distance from "a" to "b" includes a _____ and _____ displacement.

3. W1 passes below me in ____/____ second.

4. W2 passes below me in ____ / ____ second.

5. Each wavelength is _____ meters.

6. Every second, _____ waves pass below me.

7. The frequency of waves passing below me is _____ per second.

The formula for finding the speed of a wave is: **Speed = frequency*wavelength** or **s = f*wl**

8. In the formula, frequency is the same as the _____ of waves passing below where you are standing on the dock.

9. In the formula, the length of each wave from "a" to "b" is _____ meters.

Complete the formula to find the speed of the waves.

10. Speed = ____ * ____ = _____ **meters per second.**

Name _____ Date _____

SOUND

Every sound begins with a vibration. It is the vibration that creates the sound that is heard. When the vibration occurs, the air around the object creates waves in the air. These waves move through the air as sound waves. These sound waves are **longitudinal waves**. One of the definite characteristics associated with longitudinal waves is the back-and-forth movement of air molecules as the sound wave moves through the air (refer to diagram of longitudinal wave on page 54).

Sound waves move as **compressions** or places where the medium (air) is pressed together and places where the medium (air) is spread out.

Sound waves can pass through many different kinds of material. Some material will transmit the sound better than others. Liquids, solids, and gases all transmit sound waves.

Sound waves travel at an approximate speed of 1,100 feet per second in air. However, the speed of sound is affected by the temperature and humidity of the air. Sound will travel more rapidly in warm, moist air than in cool, dry air.

1. A meter is approximately 3.28 feet, so 1,100 feet per second is _____ meters per second.

A thunderstorm with lightning and thunder at location "A" is seen by Emily, Megan, and Stephany at location "B". Answer the questions that follow. Fill in the blank or circle the correct answer.

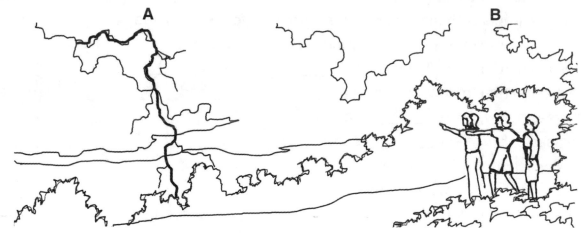

2. Find the number of feet Emily, Megan, and Stephany are from the thunderstorm if they see a flash of lightning and five seconds later hear the thunder. _____ feet

3. A mile equals 5,280 feet. Emily, Megan, and Stephany are approximately   (a) 3   (b) 8   (c) 1   (d) 10   miles from the thunderstorm.

4. A meter is approximately 3.28 feet. They are _____ meters from the thunderstorm.

5. One thousand meters equals one kilometer. Emily, Megan, and Stephany are approximately (a) 1.5   (b) 1.6   (c) 2.5   (d) 2.6   kilometers from the thunderstorm.

Name _____ Date _____

SOUND: WHAT DO YOU THINK?

Emily, Megan, and Stephany were helping time runners at a track meet. Megan and Emily each had a stopwatch and were at the finish line to record the speed of the winner. Stephany started the runners using a gun with blank shells. Emily started her stopwatch when she heard the sound of the gun. Megan started her stopwatch when she saw the smoke from the gun.

1. In the blanks below, explain which one had the most accurate measure of the winner's speed. Be sure to explain why.

_____

_____

_____

_____

_____

_____

_____

_____

2. In the previous exercise, Emily, Megan, and Stephany saw the lightning before they heard the thunder. How do you explain the difference between the time they saw the lightning and heard the thunder?

_____

_____

_____

_____

_____

_____

_____

_____

_____

57

Name _____   Date _____

LIGHT

REFLECTION

Light travels in a straight line. When light hits rough objects, it is **diffused.** The light rays are scattered and reflected in many directions. However, when light hits a shiny surface, it is not scattered. The light rays are **reflected** in a predictable manner. Reflected light has changed directions. When an **incoming ray "I"** strikes the mirror below at point "x", it behaves in a predictable manner. The incoming ray "I" is reflected back along the path "R".

When an incoming ray is reflected from a surface, the **angle of incidence** always equals the **angle of reflection.** If the angle of incidence is known, the angle of reflection can be found.

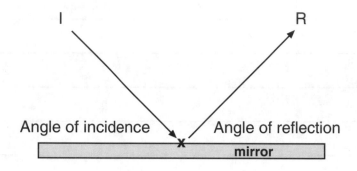

Answer the following. A protractor will be needed for this exercise.

1. The angle of incidence in the diagram above is _____ °.

2. The angle of reflection in the diagram above is _____ °.

3. In the space below, draw a ray of light striking a surface at an angle of 20°.

4. Label the ray in #3 **incoming ray.**

5. In the space below, draw a ray of light that shows the angle of reflection for #3.

6. Label the ray in #5 **reflected ray.**

7. Write the letters A.I. to locate the angle of incidence.

8. Write the letters A.R. to locate the angle of reflection.

Name _____ Date _____

LIGHT (CONTINUED)

REFRACTION

Just as light behaves in a predictable way when striking a plane surface, light also behaves in a predictable way when passing from one **medium** to another. For example, light behaves in a predictable way when passing from the medium of air to the medium of water. In this case, the light rays are **refracted**.

The diagram below shows an incoming ray of light striking the surface of the water. The incoming ray is marked "I". The refracted ray is marked "R". The dashed line represents a reference point referred to as **normal,** and it is marked "N".

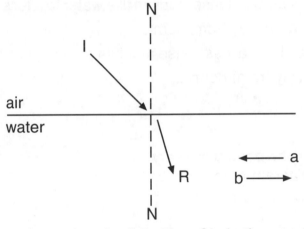

Refer to the diagram above and answer the following. Circle the correct choice.

1. Water is (denser/less dense) than air.

2. When the incoming ray "I" strikes the surface of water, the refracted ray "R" is refracted (toward/ away from) normal.

3. Arrow ("a"/"b") shows the direction of refraction in the above diagram.

In the diagram below, the light moves from water to air. The refracted ray is marked "R". Normal is marked "N". The light source is below the water, so the incoming ray is coming from the light below the water into the air.

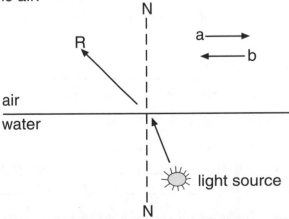

Name _____ Date _____

LIGHT (CONTINUED)

Refer to the diagram on the previous page and answer the following. Circle the correct choice.

4. Air is (denser/less dense) than water.

5. When the incoming ray "I" leaves the water and enters the air, the refracted ray "R" is refracted (toward/away from) normal.

6. Arrow ("a"/"b") shows the direction of refraction in the diagram above.

Refer to both diagrams on the previous page and answer the following. Circle the correct choice.

7. When a ray of light moves from a dense medium like water to a less dense medium like air, the refracted ray will bend (toward/away from) normal.

8. When a ray of light moves from a less dense medium to a medium that is more dense, the ray of light will bend (toward/away from) normal.

What Do You Think?

An individual sees a rock on the bottom of a very clear brook. Refer to the diagram at the right to complete the next exercise.

9. If the individual wanted to pick up the rock, show where you think the rock is actually located. Draw the rock to locate it accurately on the bottom of the brook.

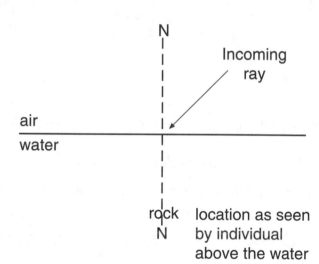

SPEED OF LIGHT

Light travels at an approximate speed of 186,000 miles per second or 300,000 kilometers per second. Light is very interesting and important to humanity. The moon is approximately 250,000 miles from the earth.

1. Write 186,000 in scientific notation. _____

2. Light travels the distance from the moon in approximately   (a) less than one second
(b) between one and two seconds   (c) over two seconds   (d) one minute.

3. Write 250,000 in scientific notation. _____

4. A kilometer is 1.6 of a mile. Light travels _____ kilometers from the moon to the earth.

5. In sixty seconds, light will travel (a) _____ miles or (b) _____ kilometers.

Name _____ Date _____

Understanding Magnetism

For centuries, man has known about magnets. Early man found that some kinds of rocks were magnetic. **Magnetite** is a rock that is naturally magnetic. Early man found that these magnetic rocks would always point to the North Star. The North Star was referred to as the lode star, and so magnetic rocks came to be called **lodestones**.

Magnets have definite characteristics. The ends of the magnets are **poles**. Magnets, when hung by a string, will naturally line up in a north-and-south direction. If allowed to move freely, one pole will always point north and the other will always point south. Therefore, one pole is a **north-seeking pole** and the other is a **south-seeking pole**. Another characteristic of magnets is that unlike poles attract each other and like poles repel one another. If a magnet is broken into pieces, each piece will still act as a magnet.

Unlike poles attract each other

Like poles repel one another

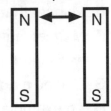

A magnetic bar can be used to magnetize some other metals. Iron and steel are two materials that can be easily magnetized. The steel or iron bar can be magnetized by stroking the bar in one direction with the magnet.

Iron filings are often used to demonstrate properties of magnets. Iron filings will attach to the poles of the magnet. The filings can be used to show that a **magnetic field** exists around each pole of the magnet. The filings can be made to become arranged in curved lines that illustrate the magnetic field around each pole.

A magnet can be used to pick up a chain of objects like paper clips or tacks. Each of the paper clips or tacks is attracted even though only one is actually in contact with the magnet. Magnetism has been **induced** into the clips or tacks attached to each other. Once the clip or tack attached to the magnet is removed, the other clips and tacks lose the magnetism.

Induced Magnetism

Name _____ Date _____

Understanding Magnetism (continued)

Some magnets like magnetite are **permanent magnets**. These magnets remain magnetized for long periods of time. **Temporary magnets** are those like iron and steel bars that have been magnetized by rubbing them with a permanent magnet like magnetite.

The earth has a magnetic field that acts like a giant magnet. One center of magnetism is known as the **magnetic North Pole**. The other is the **magnetic South Pole**. When suspended on a string, a magnet will align itself with the magnetic North and South poles.

Match the definitions in Column B with the terms in Column A.

COLUMN A

_____ 1. Magnetic lines of force

_____ 2. Magnetic North Pole

_____ 3. Permanent magnet

_____ 4. Magnetite

_____ 5. Magnetic South Pole

_____ 6. Temporary magnet

_____ 7. Lodestone

_____ 8. Induced magnetism

COLUMN B

A. Name given to magnetic rocks that point toward the North Star

B. Naturally magnetic rock

C. Magnets will naturally align north toward it.

D. Magnets will naturally align south toward it.

E. Magnet that remains magnetized for a long time

F. Magnet that has been magnetized by rubbing with a permanent magnet

G. Curved magnetic field around each pole of a magnet

H. An example of this is a string of paper clips magnetized by one clip attracted to a magnet.

Name _____ Date _____

Understanding Electricity
MEASUREMENT OF ELECTRICITY

Many things we use are measured. The number of gallons of gas used by a car to travel a certain distance, the number of gallons of water used each month in homes, and the number of pounds of fruit bought are examples of measurements that are commonly made. The electricity used in homes must be measured also. To learn about measuring electricity, one must learn the meaning of terms like **amperes, volts, watts,** and **kilowatts.**

Ampere is the measurement used to determine the flow of electrons past a certain point in a given time period. It is common to speak of the gallons of gas it takes to get from Point A to Point B. The question is, "How many gallons?". This is the same question amperes answers for us: how many electrons flow past a point. **The flow of electrons is the electric current stated in amperes.**

When measuring **volts,** think of speed or pressure. When the water faucet is turned on, the water pressure determines how rapidly and with what force the water will flow. **Voltage is the speed with which electrons travel past a given point.** A large flow of current is a high pressure or voltage.

Watts are used to measure how much power is used at a given time. To find the number of watts, both volts and amperes must be used. To measure watts, one multiplies volts times amperes. The formula is **watts = volts*amperes**. One watt is a very small amount of power. Therefore, it is common to use the term kilowatt when measuring the electrical power used. One thousand watts equals one kilowatt.

Watt-hours and **kilowatt-hours** are terms used to tell how much electrical power has been used. One watt used for one hour is one watt-hour. To find the number of watt-hours, the number of watts used must be multiplied by the number of hours. When a total of 1,000 watt-hours has been reached, it is equal to one kilowatt-hour. **One thousand watt-hours equals one kilowatt-hour.**

To measure watts, **multiply the watts used by the hours used and find the watt-hours.** A 75-watt bulb used for 2 hours becomes **watt*hours** or **75*2 = 150 watt-hours**.

Solve the following.

1. A lamp with a 100-watt bulb is on for 3 hours. Watt-hours = _____

2. A lamp with a 25-watt bulb is on for 2 hours. Watt-hours = _____

3. A lamp with a 60-watt bulb is on for 2 hours. Watt-hours = _____

One thousand watt-hours equals one kilowatt-hour.
Example: A 100-watt bulb used for 10 hours equals 100 watts*10 = 1,000 watt-hours = 1 kilowatt-hour.

Solve the following.

4. A lamp with a 100-watt bulb must be on for _____ hours to equal 1 kilowatt-hour.

5. A lamp with a 25-watt bulb must be on for _____ hours to equal 1 kilowatt-hour.

6. A lamp with a 60-watt bulb must be on for _____ hours to equal 3 kilowatt-hours.

Name _____   Date _____

DETERMINING THE COST OF ELECTRICITY

Many people pay an electricity bill each month. The amount paid depends on the number of kilowatt-hours used. The amount the electric companies charge for each kilowatt-hour is called the **rate.**

Example:The rate charged by the electric company is 8 cents per kilowatt-hour used. To determine the monthly cost, 8 cents must be multiplied by the number of kilowatt-hours used for the month. The 8 cents must be written as the decimal 0.08. If a homeowner used 1,000 kilowatt-hours for a month, then the amount charged would be 0.08*1,000 = $80.00.

Solve the following. Fill in the blank or circle the correct answer.

For the following problems, the kilowatt-hours used are 2,000 and the rate is 8 cents per kilowatt-hour.

1. Eight cents written in decimal form is   (a) 0.08   (b) 0.8   (c) 0.008   (d) 8.0.

2. To find the amount of the electricity bill, 2,000 must be multiplied by _____.

3. The amount of the electricity bill will be $ _____.

For the following problems, the kilowatt-hours used are 3,500 and the rate is 8 $\frac{1}{2}$ cents per kilowatt-hour.

4. Eight and one-half cents written in decimal form is   (a) 8.05   (b) 0.85   (c) 0.085   (d) 8.5.

5. To find the amount of the electricity bill, (a)_____ must be multiplied by (b)_____.

6. The amount of the electricity bill will be $ _____ .

Each of the following are common household appliances. The number of watts used by a given household appliance will vary for different manufacturers. For the following activity, the common household appliances listed below are shown with the watt-hours that might be used.

Toaster 500 watts   **Television 400 watts**   **Refrigerator 250 watts**
Clothes Dryer   2,000 watts   **Radio   60 watts**

To find the cost of operating an appliance for one kilowatt-hour, divide 1,000 by the watts the appliance will use each hour.

Example: A certain brand of coffee maker uses 500 watts per hour. How long will it take for the coffee maker to use one kilowatt-hour? Divide 1,000 (1,000 watts equals one kilowatt-hour) by 500 (watts used per hour by the coffee maker).

1,000/500 = 2 hours   A coffee maker using 500 watts per hour will use 1 kilowatt-hour in 2 hours of use.

Name _____ Date _____

DETERMINING THE COST OF ELECTRICITY (CONTINUED)

Solve the following: Find the number of hours each appliance can be used to equal one kilowatt-hour.

7. A toaster using 500 watts per hour for _____ hours will equal one kilowatt-hour.

8. A television using 400 watts per hour for _____ hours will equal one kilowatt-hour.

9. A refrigerator using 250 watts per hour for_____ hours will equal one kilowatt-hour.

10. A clothes dryer using 2,000 watts per hour for _____ hours will equal one kilowatt-hour.

11. A radio using 60 watts per hour for_____ hours will equal one kilowatt-hour.

Read the selection below and solve the following.

Emily enjoys listening to the radio. She leaves her radio on 20 hours every day. However, she actually listens to the radio only five hours per day. Emily's radio uses 50 watts per hour. The electricity rate charged is 10 cents per kilowatt-hour.

12. After playing   (a) 1   (b) 5   (c) 20   (d) 100   hours, Emily's radio uses one kilowatt-hour.

13. Emily's radio is using   (a) 1   (b) 5   (c) 20   (d) 100   kilowatt-hours per day.

14. The cost for playing the radio is (a) 10   (b) 20   (c) 50   (d) 30   cents per day.

15. The cost for playing the radio for 30 days is   (a) 5   (b) 20   (c) 8   (d) 3   dollars.

16. The cost for playing the radio is $ _____ for one year.

17. Emily could save $ _____ each year if she turned the radio off when she was not actually listening to it.

Name _____ Date _____

SERIES AND PARALLEL WIRING

In wiring, the terms **electrical circuit, parallel wiring,** and **series wiring** are used. An **electrical circuit** includes the wiring, switches, fuses, battery, or other source of electricity that makes the electrical current move through the wire and makes refrigerators, televisions, radios, and light bulbs work. An electrical current may be designed so the wiring is in **series** or **parallel.**

The diagram below shows a circuit wired in series.

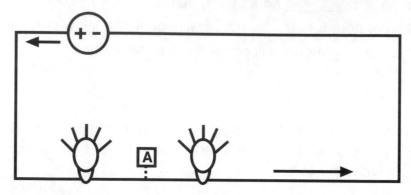
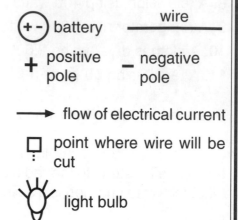

Electrical diagrams use symbols for the main components of the circuit. Refer to the diagram above and answer the following questions.

1. The wires connecting the batteries are wired from: (circle one)   (a) negative pole to positive pole   (b) positive pole to negative pole.

2. In the space at the right, draw the symbol for the battery.

3. In the space at the right, draw the symbol for the light bulb.

4. In the space at the right, draw the symbol for the wire.

What Do You Think?

5. The wire is cut at "A". On the blanks below, tell what will happen.

_____

_____

6. When a circuit is wired in series: (circle one)   (a) there are many paths for the electricity to flow through   (b) there is only one path for the electricity to flow through.

7. When a circuit is wired in series, a broken wire at any place in the circuit will result in: (circle one)
   (a) all appliances or lights on the circuit not operating
   (b) some of the appliances and lights on the circuit not operating.

66

Name _____ Date _____

SERIES AND PARALLEL WIRING (CONTINUED)

The diagram below is a circuit wired in parallel.

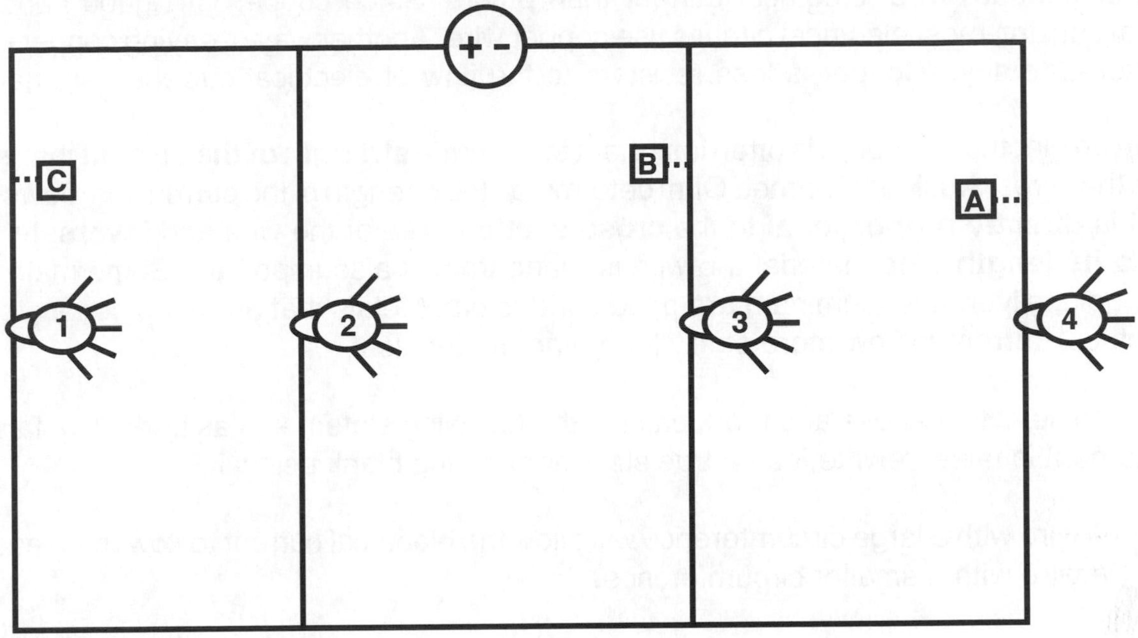

8. If the circuit is cut at Point A, which light bulb will stop working? _____

9. If the circuit is cut at Point B, which light bulb will stop working? _____

10. If the circuit is cut at Point C, which light bulb will stop working? _____

11. On the blanks below, explain why an electrical circuit wired in parallel might be better than an electrical circuit wired in series.

_____

_____

_____

_____

Name _____ Date _____

STRENGTH OF ELECTRICAL CURRENT

It is important that the electrical current flows through the wire in the circuit. Some metals are better conductors of electrical current than others. Since copper is a good conductor of electrical current, most electrical circuits use copper wire. Another way of saying copper is a good conductor is to say, "Copper is less resistant to the flow of electrical current than many other metals."

In an electrical circuit, it is often important to know the **strength of the current** that is flowing through the wires. A scientist named Ohm determined the strength of the current that flows through a circuit is **directly proportional** to the **cross-section area** of the wire and **inversely proportional to its length.** The material the wire is made from is also important. Some materials like copper, gold, silver, and aluminum are good conductors. Metals that are good conductors allow the electrical current to flow more easily than other materials.

Refer to the selection above and mark each of the following statements as true (T) or false (F). If the statement is false, rewrite it as a true statement on the blank below it.

_____ 1. A wire with a large circumference will allow the electrical current to flow more easily than a wire with a smaller circumference.

_____

_____

_____ 2. An electrical current will move more easily through a wire that is three feet long than through one that is one foot long.

_____

_____

OHM'S LAW

Ohm's Law states the **circumference** of the wire, the **length** of the wire, and the **material** the wire is made from **determine the resistance** in an electrical circuit. Ohm's Law measures the resistance to the flow of electricity in a circuit.

Lamps, refrigerators, and other appliances also resist the flow of electricity through a circuit. The resistance to the flow of electricity by the appliances is used to make appliances and light bulbs operate. The filament in a light bulb is resistant to the flow of electrical current. The filament resists the flow of electricity and becomes hotter. Finally, the heat from the electrical current causes the filament to glow and furnish light.

3. According to Ohm's Law, which of the following wires will offer the greatest resistance to the flow of an electrical current? Assume all the wires are made of the same material. Circle the correct choice.

A. ⊂◯_____⊃   B. ⊂◯_____⊃

C. ⊂◯_____⊃   D. ⊂◯_____⊃

Name _____ Date _____

STRENGTH OF ELECTRICAL CURRENT (CONTINUED)

4. On the blanks below, explain how you chose your answer in #3.

_____

_____

5. Select the wire below that you think will be the best to use in an electrical circuit. In the blank below each wire, tell why you think it is or is not the best for an electrical circuit.

A) 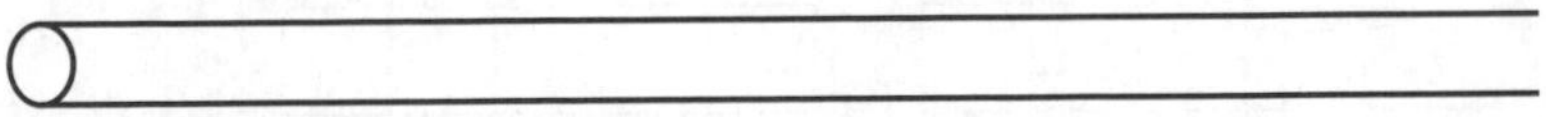 ⊙—————————————————

Wire is made of lead. _____

_____

B) 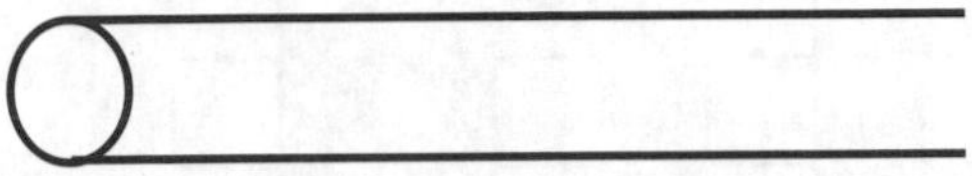 ◯—————————————

Wire is made of copper. _____

_____

C)  ⊙———————————————

Wire is made of copper. _____

_____

To answer the following questions, refer to the in-series and in-parallel diagrams on pages 66 and 67. Circle the correct answers.

6. In the diagrams, the source(s) of electrical power are   (a) batteries   (b) light bulbs.

7. In the diagrams, the   (a) batteries   (b) light bulbs   are the resistance.

8. Ohm's Law measures   (a) resistance   (b) current   in an electrical system.

ALTERNATING AND DIRECT CURRENT

Current that flows through an electrical circuit may be **direct** current or **alternating** current. **Direct current flows one direction in the circuit.** The current always flows from the negative to the positive pole in the circuit. **Alternating current flows first one direction and then reverses to flow the other direction in the circuit.** The alternating current reverses the electrical flow from the positive to negative pole and then from negative to positive. The change from negative to positive and from positive to negative is known as a **cycle**. The cycle (change in direction of electrical flow) occurs so many times per second.

Name _____ Date _____

ELECTRICITY CROSSWORD PUZZLE

Use the clues on page 71 to complete the crossword puzzle below. Answers may be found in the previous pages on electricity or other source books with electrical information.

Name _____ Date _____

ELECTRICITY CROSSWORD PUZZLE CLUES

Use these clues to complete the crossword puzzle on page 70.

ACROSS

1. Refers to electric current when electrons flow in one direction and then flow in the opposite direction in the wire (two words)

8. The change from negative to positive and from positive to negative in an alternating current

9. An electric circuit where electrons must follow one path (two words)

12. The speed with which electrons travel past a given point. The symbol is **V**.

14. Measures the amount of resistance that limits the flow of current. The symbol is Ω.

17. Works like a fuse to keep the electrical system from becoming overloaded (two words)

18. A lightning rod is an example. It is used to let electricity travel into the earth.

19. The symbol for it is **R**.

DOWN

2. Copper is an example because electric charges move through it easily.

3. Refers to the flow of electrons through a wire (two words)

4. Materials like wood and paper that electrons cannot easily move through

5. It is used to prevent overloading of an electric circuit.

6. A unit of electrical power; determined by multiplying volts times amperes

7. Equals 1,000 watts

10. It is used to store potential electrical energy. In an automobile, they are 6 or 12 volt.

11. An instrument that shows temperature by changing heat energy into electric energy

13. A battery with a paste-like mixture of chemicals (two words)

15. An electric circuit where electrons may follow more than one path (two words)

16. Refers to electric current when electrons always flow in the same direction in the wire (two words)

20. Unit of measure that determines the flow of electrons past a certain point in a given period of time; the symbol is **A.**

Answer Keys

Understanding Matter (page 1)
1) Mass and weight are not the same; mass is the amount of matter, while weight is the force of gravity.
2) The mass of an object is the same on Earth's surface as at 1,000 feet.
3) An object on Earth's surface has both mass and weight.

Measurement of Mass (page 2)
CHART I
2) 2; 4.4
3) 3; 6.6
4) 3.5; 7.7
5) 4,000; 8.8
6) 6,500; 14.3
7) 8,000; 8
8) 1.1
9) 10; 0.22
10) 1; 0.0022

Measurement of Weight (pages 3–4)
CHART II
2) 9,800
3) 49,000
4) 98,000
5) 980,000

6) 980,000
7) 9.8

CHART III	CHART IV
9) 98	14) 45
10) 980	15) 450 (N)
11) 4,900	16) 675 (N)
12) 9,800	17) 900 (N)

18) Teacher check

Comparing Measurements of Weight (page 4)
1) 2.2	7) 22
2) 9.8	8) 98
3) 4.4	9) 980
4) 19.6	10) 220
5) 11	11) grams; kilograms
6) 49	12) dynes; newtons

Density (page 5)
1a) 3 b) 4 c) 5 d) 60
2a) 216 b) feet
3a) 30 b) cubic
4a) 54 b) cubic
5a) 280 b) cubic c) meters

Comparing Volume, Density, and Weight (page 6)
1) the same; the material (matter) is the same.
2) the same; their volumes are the same.
3) different; the materials (matter) is different.
4) different; the densities are different.
5) the same; the material (matter) is the same.
6) different; the volumes are different.

Reviewing the Properties of Matter (page 7)
1) matter	6) weight
2) mass	7) gravity
3) mass	8) gravitational attraction
4) weight	9) force
5) mass	

10)

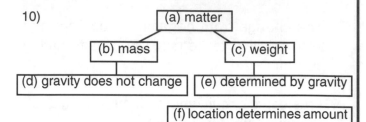

11) Teacher check/discuss
12) Teacher check/discuss

Understanding How Numbers Are Written in Science (page 8)
1a) 210	2b) 10^2
b) 6,420	d) 10^4
c) 96,540	e) 10^5
d) 1,600,410	f) 10^6
e) 3,500,800	

How to Write in Scientific Notation (page 9)
1) 3.6×10^7	5) 1.28×10^7
2) 6.69×10^7	6) 1.205×10^8
3) 9.3×10^7	7) 1.198×10^8
4) 1.41×10^8	8) 5.11×10^7
	9) 4.95×10^7
	10) 2.34×10^6

Understanding Mass and Gravity (pages 10–11)
1a) +; Gravitational force is less at 30,000 feet, so the person weighs less at 30,000 feet.
 b) -; The mass does not change.
 c) -; Gravitational force is less at 30,000 feet, so the person weighs less at 30,000 feet.
 d) +; Gravitational force is less at 40,000 feet than at 30,000 feet, so the person weighs less at 40,000 feet.
 e) +; The mass does not change.
2a) decrease; b) away from; c) will not
3)   (e) 80
                    (d) 90
                    (c) 100
                    (b) 120
Earth's surface (a) 140

4a) less
  b) less
  c) the same as
  d) 1/6
  e) 1/6
  f) are

Questions About Gravity (page 12)
Teacher check written responses

1) yes	4) yes
2) yes	5) yes
3) yes	6) no

How Gravity and Time Affect the Distance and Speed of a Falling Object (pages 13–14)

2) 3; 3; 9	7) 1
3) 4; 4; 4; 16	8) 144
4) 1; 1; 1; 1	9) 400
5) 5; 5; 5; 25	10) 4
6) 6; 6; 6; 36	11) 16

12) From left to right in grid:
1, 2, 2, 2, 3, 3, 3, 3, 3, 4, 4, 4, 4, 4, 4, 4, 5, 5, 5, 5, 5, 5, 5, 5, 5

14) 16; 4; 64
15) 16; 9; 144
16) 16; 16; 256
17) 16; 25; 400

Using the Metric System in Distance and Speed Problems (page 15)

2) d; 4.9; 4; 19.6	6) 5
3) d; 4.9; 9; 44.1	7) 10
4) d; 4.9; 16; 78.4	8) 15
5) d; 4.9; 25; 122.5	9) 29

10) 64
11) 129
12) 579
13) 788
14) 289
15) 321

How Gravity and Time Affect the Speed of a Falling Object (pages 16–17)
1) 64
2) 160 feet
3) 256 feet per second
4) 64
5) 400
6) 1,024
7) 19.6
8) 49 meters
9) 78.4 meters per second
10) 19.5

11) 122
12) 312.2

Reviewing Gravity, Time, Distance, and Speed (pages 18–20)
1) Stephany
2) Stephany
3) Stephany, Emily, Megan
4) 16
5) 64
6) 64
7) 64
8) 144
9) 64
10) 64
11) 320
12) 464

Colors appearing right to left in grid
A: R, B, B, B, Y, Y, Y, Y, Y, O, O, O, O, O, O, O, Bl, Bl, Bl, Bl, Bl, Bl, Bl, Bl, Bl
B: R, R, R, R, R, B, B, B, Y, Y, Y, Y, Y, O, O, O, O, O, O, O, Bl, Bl, Bl, Bl, Bl, Bl, Bl, Bl, Bl
C: R, B, B, B, Y, Y, Y, Y, Y, O, O, O, O, O, O, O, Bl, Bl, Bl, Bl, Bl, Bl, Bl, Bl, Bl

13) Teacher check
14) 16
15) b
16) a

17) 64; 19.5	21) 16; 4.9
18) 128; 39	22) 64; 19.5
19) 192; 58.5	23) 144; 43.9
20) 256; 78	24) 256; 78

Colors appearing right to left in grid
D: R, B, B, B, Y, Y, Y, Y, Y, O, O, O, O, O, O, O
E: R, R, R, R, B, B, B, B, Y, Y, Y, Y, O, O, O, O

25) d
26) Teacher check
27) b
28) Teacher check

Drawing a Parabola (page 21)
1) Teacher discuss/check
2) Teacher discuss/check
3) c
4) parabola

Plotting a Parabola (page 22)
1b) 2 c) 2 d) 2
2b) 128; 4 c) 128; 4 d) 4
3a) 320; 32 b) 320/32; 10; c) 320; 32; 10 d) 10

Learning How High the Object Will Be After Each Second (page 23)
1) Teacher check
2) parabola
3) 80
4) 128
5) 144
6) 128
7) 80
8) 3
9) 3
10) Teacher check/discuss

More Parabola Practice (page 24)
1a) 4
 b) 256 feet
2a) 4
 b) 78.4 meters
Teacher check graph
3–4) Teacher check/discuss
5) a parabola

Reviewing What Has Been Learned (page 25)
1) C
2) E
3) F
4) B
5) H
6) G
7) A
8) D

Reviewing the Effects of Gravity (pages 25–26)
1) Teacher check/discuss
2a) 96; 16; 1; 80
 b) 6
 c) 6; 6; 288
3a) 96; 8; 1; 88
 b) 12
 c) 12; 12; 576
4) a
5) b
6) $\frac{1}{2}$

Understanding Motion (pages 27–28)
1) 5 miles per hour
2) 500 miles; hour
3) 10 yards; second
4) 10 meters; second
5) 60 kilometers; hour

6) 5 miles; south
7) 500 miles; southwest
8) 60 kilometers; north
9) 1

10) 50
11) 50
12) 0.025; second

More Motion Notions (page 29)
1) accelerating
2) average
3) decelerated
4) momentum
5) accelerated
6) decelerate
7) centripetal
8) accelerated
9) decelerated
10) average
11) speed

Learning More About Acceleration and Deceleration (pages 30–31)
1) acceleration
2) terminal speed
3) initial speed
4) beginning
5) ending
6) change

7) $10 = \frac{60 - 30}{3}$

8) per
10) $10 = \frac{50 - 20}{3}$ (10 mph per minute)

11a) 32 b) 80 c) $16 = \frac{80 - 32}{3}$ (16 kph per minute)

12) 17.6 feet per second; second
13) 15 feet per second; second
14) 9.6 feet per second; second
15) 10 meters per second; second
16) 11 feet per second; second
17) 15 meters per second; second
18) 5 mph
19) 25 mph
20a) 100; hour
 b) 60; hour
 c) 10; minute
 d) 62.5
 e) 37.5
 f) 6,25 mph; minute

Speed, Velocity, and Displacement (page 32)
1) b
2) c
3) a
4) east
5) 100 miles east of origin

6) 50 miles per hour east
7) north
8) 100 miles north of origin
9) 50 miles per hour north
10) south
11) 100 miles south of origin
12) 50 miles per hour south
13–15) Teacher check

Identifying Speed or Velocity (page 33)
1) v
2) s
3) s
4) v
5) v
6) s
7) s

Speed and Velocity in Miles and Kilometers (page 33)
2) 10 mph; 16 kph
3) 50 mph; 1,600; 80 kph
4) 50 hrs.; 50 hrs.
5) 50 mph; 800; 10 hrs.; 80 kph
6) 5; 2.5 mph

Determining Speed, Time, and Distance (page 34)
1a) distance b) speed c) time
2) c
3) 8 hours
4a) speed b) time c) distance
5) b
6) 2,000 miles
7a) distance b) time c) speed
8) a
9) 60 miles per hour

Using Graphs to Illustrate Distance and Time (page 35)
1) c; d) 1
2) c; d) 8
3) b
4) 200
5) 25
6) Teacher check
7) 300
8) Teacher check
9) 275

Using Diagrams to Illustrate Speed and Velocity (page 36)
1) 25
2) east
3) a
4) 56.25
5) east

6) b
7) 37.5
8) south
9) b

Motion Matching (page 36)
1) B
2) F
3) E
4) G
5) C
6) A
7) D

Understanding Scalar and Vector Quantities (page 37)
1) Teacher check
2a) 120 b) north
3a) 160 b) west
4a) 200 b) southeast

Using Vectors to Plot Displacement (pages 38–39)
Teacher check vector drawing
1) 200
2) a
3) d
4) a
5) c
6) 175
7) c
8) c
9) c
10) b
11) 275
12) a
13) d
14) a
15) a

The Scientific Meaning of Work (page 40)
1) +; Both statements should be checked.
2) +; Both statements should be checked.
3) -; Only the first statement should be checked.
4) -; Neither statement should be checked.
5) -; Only the first statement should be checked.
6) Teacher check

Measuring Work in the English and Metric Systems (page 41)
1) force
2) distance
3) c
4) a
5) c
6) b
7) 50
8) 91.4

Reviewing the Measurement of Work (page 42)
1) work
2) foot-pounds
3) newton-meters

4) English/metric
5) metric/English
6) force
7) distance
8) simple machines

9) D
10) E
11) F
12) A
13) C
14) B

15a) 50 b) 2 c) 50; 2 d) 100
16a) 140 b) 5 c) 140; 5 d) 700 foot-pounds
17a) 120 b) 10 c) w = 120 * 10 d) 1,200 foot-pounds

The Scientific Meaning of Power (pages 43–44)
1) power
2) work
3) work
4) power
5a) agree; work was performed when the object moved a specific distance.
 b) agree; the object must be moved, not just held.
6a) agree; the weights were back in the original position.
 b) agree; the weights would have been moved a specific distance and placed at a new location
 c) agree; the weights are four feet from the original position on the floor.
7) a, c, and d should have plus (+) marks
8a) agree; work done is part of the formula for determining power.
 b) agree; the formula is work = force * distance.
 c) agree; work equals force times distance.
9a) 2,200
 b) 2,200
 c) 2,200/5
 d) 440

Work and Power: What Do You Think? (page 45)
1) a
2a) False; The force and distance for all three was the same.
 b) False; The force and distance for all three was the same.
 c) True; the force and distance for all three was the same.
3a) True; Emily moved the books in a shorter period of time.
 b) True; Emily moved the books in a shorter period of time.
 c) False; Emily moved the books in a shorter period of time than Megan and Stephany.
4a) power
 b) work

Simple Machines (pages 46–47)
1) Megan; the lever increased the mechanical advantage.
2) will
3) will not
4) Stephany
5) Megan's

6) 4; 5; 0.8
7) 2; 8; 0.25

Reviewing Work, Power, and Simple Machines (page 48)
1) H
2) G
3) C
4) E
5) F
6) A
7) I
8) B
9) D

10)

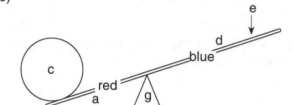

Understanding Solids, Liquids, and Gases (page 49)
1) G
2) S
3) S
4) L
5) G
6) L
7) L
8) S

9) Teacher check

Understanding Temperature and Heat (page 50)
1) energy
2) temperature
3) solid
4) liquid
5) gas

Thermometers (page 50)
1) B
2) C
3) D
4) E
5) A

Measuring Temperature With Fahrenheit, Celsius, and Kelvin Scales (page 51)
1) Fahrenheit
2) Celsius
3) Kelvin
4) Celsius
5) K
6) Fahrenheit
7) 212
8) Celsius
9) 100

10) b
11) c
12) d
13) d
14) b

Temperature Scale Conversions (page 52)

1) 32	7) 77; 45; 25
2) 50	8) 212; 32; 9; 180; 5; 9; 100°
3) 18	9) 25; 45; 77
4) 10	10) 0; 9; 5; 32; 0; 32; 32°
5) 1.8	
6) d	

Understanding Wave Action (page 53)
1) air
2) water

3) speeds
4) medium
5) distance
6) type
7) travel
8) Sound
9) Light
10) air
11) water

Longitudinal and Transverse Waves (page 54)
1) B
2) A
3) G
4) F
5) H
6) I
7) D
8) E
9) J
10) C

Wave Speed (page 55)
1) crest; trough
2) maximum and minimum

3) 1/2
4) 1/2
5) 2
6) 2
7) 2
8) number
9) 2
10) 2 * 2 = 4

Sound (page 56)
1) 335
2) 5,500
3) c
4) 1,677
5) b

Sound: What Do You Think? (page 57)
Teacher check answers

Light
Reflection (page 58)
1) 45°
2) 45°
3–8) Teacher check diagram

Refraction (pages 59–60)
1) denser
2) toward
3) "a"

4) less dense
5) away from
6) "b"

7) away from
8) toward
9) Teacher check diagram. Rock should be drawn slightly to the left of normal line.

Speed of Light (page 60)
1) 1.86×10^5
2) b
3) 2.5×10^5
4) 400,000
5a) 11,160,000 b) 18,000,000

Understanding Magnetism (page 62)
1) G
2) C
3) E
4) B
5) D
6) F
7) A
8) H

Measurement of Electricity (page 63)
1) 300
2) 50
3) 120
4) 10
5) 40
6) 50

Determining the Cost of Electricity (pages 64–65)
1) a
2) 0.08
3) $160.00
4) c
5a) 3,500 b) 0.085
6) 297.50

7) 2
8) 2.5
9) 4
10) 0.5
11) 16.66

12) c
13) a
14) a
15) d
16) $36.50
17) $27.38

Understanding Series and Parallel Wiring (pages 66–67)
1) b
2–4) Teacher check
5) Answers should include: The lights will go out, or the electricity will not flow.
6) b
7) a
8) 4
9) 3
10) 1
11) Electricity continues to flow and furnish power to some parts of the circuit.

Strength of Electrical Current (pages 68–69)
1) T
2) F; An electrical current will move more easily through a wire that is one foot long than one that is three feet long.

3) Wire B
4) Answers will vary but should include the following information: Wire B has the smallest circumference and is the longest wire.
5) Teacher check/discuss. Wire B should be chosen as the best to use in an electrical circuit because it has the greatest circumference, it is shortest, and it is made of copper.
6) a
7) b
8) a

Electricity Crossword Puzzle (pages 70–71)

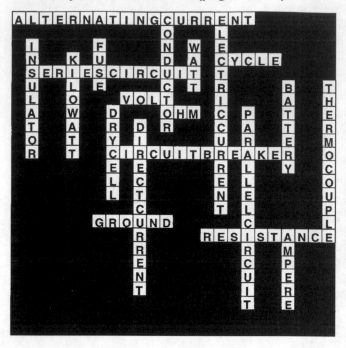